Creating Choices

Rethinking Aboriginal Policy

John Richards

Policy Study 43

C.D. Howe Institute

C.D. Howe Institute publications are available from:
Renouf Publishing Company Limited, 5369 Canotek Road, Unit 1,
Ottawa, Ontario K1J 9J3
phone: (613) 745-2665; fax: (613) 745-7660;
Internet: www.renoufbooks.com

This book is printed on recycled, acid-free paper.

Library and Archives Canada Cataloguing in Publication

Richards, John
    Creating choices : rethinking Aboriginal policy / John Richards.

(Policy study, 0832-7912 ; 43)
ISBN 0-88806-653-8

    1. Native peoples—Health and hygiene—Canada. 2. Native
peoples—Education—Canada. 3. Native peoples—Canada—Government
relations. I. C.D. Howe Institute II. Title. III. Series: Policy study
(C.D. Howe Institute) ; 43.

E92.R515 2006   305.897'071'021   C2006-900188-X

Contents

Figures

Tables

Foreword

Creating Choices is an admirable review of many of the issues that affect Aboriginal policy in Canada. John Richards, Phillips Scholar in Social Policy and Fellow-in-Residence at the C.D. Howe Institute, is one of Canada's leading analysts of these issues. His numerous papers on the subject and his deep involvement in Aboriginal policy discussions at both the federal and provincial levels are testament to his hard work to help improve the lot of Canada's Aboriginals, whether they live on- or off-reserve.

As he writes, "Canada cannot — nor should it — return to the pre–1969 White Paper world of pessimistic anthropology and its accompanying policies." Canadians have undertaken to assure that Aboriginal governments and culture survive. This book is not, however, about Aboriginal self-government; rather, it explores pragmatic policy reforms that all levels of government — federal, provincial, and Aboriginal — should be undertaking. Whatever the root causes in past history, the key immediate cause for Aboriginal poverty, Professor Richards argues, is the low level of Aboriginal education. Low education leads to low employment rates and the intergenerational perpetuation of poverty. Low education levels, low employment rates, and many Aboriginal health problems — such as diabetes — are closely interrelated.

In this book, Professor Richards offers a carefully developed analysis of Aboriginal policy, focusing on several key areas in need of reform. Among his recommendations are the following:

- reform the on-reserve Aboriginal education system, by creating province-wide or multi-band Aboriginal school boards and adopting curricula and student testing better integrated with those of provincially run schools;
- make greater use of affirmative action programs in provincial school systems to improve Aboriginal education success;
- integrate Aboriginal and provincial health care systems in order to improve the quality and management of health care for Aboriginals;

- eliminate the federal tax exemption for Aboriginals in order to improve the efficiency and equity of the tax system as it applies to Aboriginals as full citizens of Canada;
- rather than send all Indian Affairs transfers to band councils, send some portion to individual Registered Indians and allow band councils to tax reserve residents to pay for services; a move toward own-source taxation would probably do much to improve the quality of band governance;
- create an intertribal social assistance agency for each province to administer on-reserve social assistance.

These proposals are intended to permit Aboriginals to enjoy the rights and opportunities available to other Canadians. Undoubtedly, such proposals will be subject to much debate, but the objective of higher incomes and employment rates for Aboriginals is a worthy goal and one that, if achieved, would place Aboriginals in a far better position to support and maintain their communities and lifestyles.

I wish to thank the many reviewers of the manuscript who offered their valuable insights and counsel — in particular, Finn Poschmann, who steered the book through the research process. I also thank Barry Norris for his capable editing and desktop publishing of this significant book, as well as Wendy Longsworth, Diane King, and James Fleming for their contributions to the production process.

As with all C.D. Howe Institute publications, the analysis and opinions presented in this study are those of the author, and do not necessarily reflect the views of the Institute's members or Board of Directors.

Jack M. Mintz
President and
Chief Executive Officer

Preface

A small Aboriginal elite now exists, able to give voice to historical injustices. The list of injustices is long: expropriation of Aboriginal lands by European settlers and relegation of Aboriginals to small reserves on marginal land; imposition of residential schools; long-standing indifference of white Canadians to Aboriginal social outcomes in terms of education, income, and health. This history has rendered Aboriginal attitudes toward mainstream Canada equivalent to those of many black Americans toward mainstream America. In both cases, the sins of the past haunt the present.

For centuries, white settlers adopted an instinctive sense of racial superiority to Aboriginals. At some point in the 1970s, Canadians repented; since then, majority attitudes have been suffused with "white guilt." The combination of white guilt and Aboriginal anger over past history is not, however, a basis for good policy. A more substantive and pragmatic dialogue is long overdue, one that addresses what needs to be done here and now. This book is a modest contribution to such rethinking.

First, a few words on what this book is *not* about. It is not about the interpretation and implementation of treaty rights. Treaties have an important role in any discussion of policy for the three in ten Aboriginals who live on-reserve. But seven in ten now live off-reserve, and five in ten live in cities. Accordingly, this book is essentially an exploration of pragmatic strategies that all levels of government — federal, provincial, municipal, and reserve-based band councils — could employ to improve the health and education outcomes of Aboriginal Canadians, wherever they live.

In writing this book, I have been influenced by many people's ideas. Jean Allard's history of Aboriginal policy since the tabling of the federal government's 1969 White Paper is an important document, as are his ideas about "updated treaty money." Former Saskatchewan premier Allan Blakeney was well in advance of most Canadian politicians in arguing the case for institutions — such as local governments in northern Saskatchewan — in which

Aboriginals could exercise political influence. Blakeney has sustained his engagement since leaving office, consistently making the case for greater emphasis on Aboriginal employment and on the significance of the growing urban Aboriginal communities. On the subject of education policy, my colleague Aidan Vining has helped me think more clearly about what works and what does not, and why. Several years ago, I edited an animated exchange of "letters" between Alan Cairns and Tom Flanagan, both of whom have thought deeply about Aboriginal matters.

I have enjoyed the privilege of ongoing discussions about Aboriginal policy with many friends and colleagues. Here I mention Barry Anderson, Susan Anzolin, Alex Berland, Gordon Gibson, Brenda Green, Doug McArthur, Greg Marchildon, Tony Penikett, Ulrike Radermache, Guy Richards, Andy Siggner, and Pamela Sparklingeyes. Their being in this list does not, of course, imply their agreeing with my conclusions.

Another group has generously reviewed earlier drafts of this manuscript, either in whole or in part. For undertaking the task of critical reviewer, I first thank Finn Poschmann. Other reviewers were Alex Berland, Allan Blakeney, Matthew Brzozowski, Alan Cairns, Gordon Gibson, Jeremy Hull, Sheilla Jones, David Laidler, Tom and Jim McCarthy, and Greg Marchildon. Linda Wong helped assemble much of the data on Aboriginal health and education reported in Chapters 3 and 4. Mikhyla Richards undertook literature research on diabetes.

Barry Norris undertook the copy editing of the manuscript. He did his best to render the writing clear and logical. The remaining inadequacies are my responsibility, not his. He and Wendy Longsworth jointly prepared the manuscript for printing.

In outline, I have organized this book as follows. Chapter 1 relates an incident in spring 2002 of no great import, but one that reveals a good deal about the current estrangement of Aboriginals and non-Aboriginals. Chapter 2 provides a highly condensed survey of Aboriginal policy in Canada from Confederation to the 1996 Royal Commission on Aboriginal Peoples, plus an appendix summarizing statistics on Aboriginal demography. Chapters 3 and 4 are the core of the book and deal, respectively, with health and education outcomes among Aboriginals and what might be done to improve matters. Chapter 5 explores the politically charged subject of defining reasonable limits to Aboriginal political expectations. Finally, Chapter 6 immodestly poses what I think to be the policy issues to tackle if future dialogue between Aboriginals and non-Aboriginals is to bear fruit.

John Richards
November 2005

1 *Benoît v The Queen*

In 2002, Gordon Benoît, a Registered Indian of the Mikisew Cree Nation in northern Alberta, went to court to claim that, according to his treaty rights, he should be exempt from federal taxation. What should the court have decided? Before I attempt to answer, let me provide a little context.

In spring 2002, the Liberal government of British Columbia, fulfilling a 2001 election campaign promise, held a referendum on principles to guide the province in undertaking tripartite treaty negotiations with Ottawa and provincial Indian bands. The holding of such a referendum did not, however, meet with universal approval. Many Aboriginal leaders challenged the legitimacy of subjecting such matters to a vote among non-Aboriginals. Treaties, they argued, were a matter of legal interpretation of historical Aboriginal rights, or of nation-to-nation bargaining among governments. For its part, the provincial government argued that the range of issues being negotiated had become so broad as to require consultation with British Columbians more generally.

Coincident with the referendum campaign, Simon Fraser University organized a series of public lectures on Aboriginal treaty issues. One evening that spring, some 200 people — Aboriginal and

non-Aboriginal — assembled at SFU's downtown Vancouver campus to hear professors Alan Cairns and Tom Flanagan discuss the
dilemma of how to reconcile treaty rights with the obligations of
Canadian citizenship. During the coffee break, political theory and the
forthcoming referendum retreated to the background as participants
debated the rights and wrongs of Gordon Benoît's taxes. That day,
in a Federal Court Trial Division decision,[1] Benoît had won his case.

Indians living on-reserve had long been exempt from federal
taxes. However, those living off-reserve, like Benoît, had enjoyed
no general tax exemption. In support of Benoît's claim, his lawyers
referred to an 1899 report by federal treaty commissioners to the
Honourable Clifford Sifton, superintendent general of Indian Affairs,
at the time of the signing of "Treaty 8," which covers Aboriginal
peoples living in a vast region of western Canada. The commissioners wrote at length about many aspects of the treaty negotiations:[2]

> There was a marked absence of the old Indian style of oratory.
> Only among the Wood Crees were any formal speeches made,
> and these were brief....The Chipewyans confined themselves to
> asking questions and making brief arguments. They appeared to
> be more adept at cross-examination than at speech-making, and
> the Chief at Fort Chipewyan displayed considerable keenness of
> intellect and much practical sense in pressing the claims of his
> band....They seemed desirous of securing educational advantages
> for their children, but stipulated that in the matter of schools there
> should be no interference with their religious beliefs.
>
> We pointed out that the Government could not undertake to
> maintain Indians in idleness; that the same means of earning a
> livelihood would continue after the treaty as existed before it, and
> that the Indians would be expected to make use of them. We told
> them that the Government was always ready to give relief in
> cases of actual destitution, and that in seasons of distress they

1 *Benoît v The Queen*, 2002 DTC 6896.

2 The following quotations from the commissioners' report are taken from the
   decision by the Federal Court of Appeal, *The Queen v Benoît*, 2003 FCA 236,
   available online at http://decisions.fct-cf.gc.ca/fct/2003/2003fca236.shtml.

would without any special stipulation in the treaty receive such
assistance as it was usual to give in order to prevent starvation
among Indians in any part of Canada....We promised that sup-
plies of medicines would be put in the charge of persons selected
by the Government at different points, and would be distributed
free to those of the Indians who might require them.

On the matter of taxation, the commissioners reported, "We
assured them [the chiefs negotiating Treaty 8] that the treaty would
not lead to any forced interference with their mode of life, that it
did not open the way to the imposition of any tax, and there was
no fear of enforced military service." In rendering his verdict that
Benoît need not pay tax, the Federal Court Trial Division judge thus
viewed the commissioners' account as legitimate evidence to support the claim that contemporary chiefs had understood Treaty 8 to
mean no taxation of Indians within the entire territory covered by
the treaty.

All of the Aboriginals — whether Indian or Métis, Registered
Indian or not — among the audience at SFU's Vancouver campus
that spring evening in 2002 endorsed the verdict. In their view, it
was bad enough that white settlers had seized the continent and
shunted their ancestors onto small reserves. Why should they, as
Aboriginals, suffer the ongoing indignity of paying taxes to white
settler governments?

A more subtle argument turned on the importance of oral evidence. Admittedly, the written text of Treaty 8 did not specify an
absolute tax exemption, but since very few contemporary Indians
could read and write, the written document was of limited legitimacy. In their haste to obtain the acquiescence of the Indians, the
commissioners had doubtless misrepresented the treaty's provisions.
The commissioners' report to Ottawa was better evidence, some
Aboriginals at the SFU lecture argued, of what the Indians thought
they had signed than was the text of the document itself.

Many of the non-Aboriginals present that evening had lived
with and worked beside Aboriginals, but few were familiar with such
arguments. Some empathized as fellow taxpayers: if Registered

Indians had found a way to beat the tax collector, good for them. For most, however, the verdict was disturbing. Like most Canadians, the non-Aboriginals in the audience believed paying taxes to be a core obligation of citizenship. If governments were to organize decent schools and hospitals, regulate the environment, and pay old age security, citizens would need to relinquish a sizable fraction of their income in the form of taxes.

The discussion gave rise to a number of questions, some of them highly skeptical in tone. Here is a flavour of the questions and the responses that evening in Vancouver.

Should a low-income, non-Aboriginal family pay income tax while an Indian family, however rich, pays none?

The consensus among non-Aboriginals was that such a situation was fundamentally unfair. If government is to redistribute wealth from the rich to the poor — a group in which Aboriginals are over-represented — all Canadians should be taxed on a racially neutral basis. The Aboriginals, however, did not yield. Admittedly, they said, Canadians entertain an ideal of equality: those with equal incomes should pay equal taxes and those with higher incomes should pay more than those with lower incomes. But, they argued, white governments do not practise what they preach. Only when governments put an end to family trusts (as means to avoid capital gains taxes) and to the tax advantages that groups such as farmers enjoy will it be time to discuss any inequities created by *Benoît*. To attack tax privileges for Indians first was racism.

Is ongoing litigation to exempt Aboriginals from fundamental obligations of Canadian citizenship reasonable in seeking to resolve Aboriginal grievances?

By and large, the non-Aboriginals answered "No." *Benoît*, they said, was socially divisive. On-reserve Indians had a case for special treatment; increasingly, however, Indians are urban dwellers, using the same public services as everyone else. Surely, everyone must share the costs of providing these services. The Aboriginals disagreed. For them, in recent decisions — for example, *Sparrow, Delgamuukw,* and *Marshall* — the courts were simply transforming words into reality, and about time, too. Litigation was merely forcing Canadians to meet obligations they undertook when Aboriginal rights were entrenched in section 35 of the 1982 *Constitution Act,* which states:

> (1) The existing Aboriginal and treaty rights of the Aboriginal peoples of Canada are hereby recognized and affirmed.
> (2) In the [Canada] Act, "Aboriginal peoples of Canada" includes the Indian, Inuit and Métis peoples of Canada.
> (3) For greater certainty, in subsection (1) "treaty rights" includes the rights that now exist by way of land claims agreements or may be so acquired.

Should governments be negotiating new treaties between Indians and other Canadians that envisage few shared aspects of citizenship and the perpetual transfer of funds from Canadian taxpayers to "First Nations"?

The motive for this question was that, except for the northeast corner of British Columbia subject to Treaty 8, all other non-Aboriginal settlement in the province had taken place in the absence of treaties. What non-Aboriginals at the lecture had in mind was the one modern-day treaty ratified so far — namely, that with the Nisga'a, whose traditional lands lie in the northwest of the province. That treaty, whose text is longer than the *British North America Act,* envisions the phase-out of the on-reserve income tax exemption, but it also implies indefinite federal funding of the majority of services that on-reserve Nisga'a residents receive and minimal interaction with non-Aboriginal institutions.

In response to non-Aboriginal objections to a "nation-to-nation" relationship between Aboriginals and other Canadians, the Aboriginals retorted that they were here first. They had the right to govern themselves, they said — a right acknowledged in documents such as the Royal Proclamation of 1763 and now entrenched in the Canadian Constitution, and one they intended to preserve. The Nisga'a Treaty, they pointed out, was the result of voluntary negotiations between the Canadian government in Ottawa, the provincial government in Victoria, and the Nisga'a people on their lands. How could anyone object to that?

The Aboriginals drew parallels to francophone Quebec. If Quebecers could embrace separatism and still be considered Canadians, why should Aboriginals be limited to institutions in which they were a small minority? Francophone Quebecers control a National Assembly in which they legislate to protect their language and culture against assimilation. Why should Indians not enjoy band governments with the power to do the same within their territories? And why not create urban reserves with the financial means to provide services to urban Indians? For more than a century, Ottawa had ignored the spirit of treaty provisions. If Ottawa was not prepared to make good on those treaties and transfer to the Indians the lands to which they were entitled, then Ottawa should provide Aboriginals the financial means to buy land — including urban land — to which reserve status should then be extended.

In June 2003, the Federal Court of Appeal overturned *Benoît* on the grounds that the trial judge had made an unduly selective use of oral evidence. The case may well be subject to further appeal to the Supreme Court of Canada. Upon learning of the reversal, Matthew Coon Come, then national chief of the Assembly of First Nations, stated that he would

> encourage and support Treaty 8 to continue their litigation effort. The government and all Canadians have to understand that they too have benefited greatly from the Treaties which allowed them to share in the richness of the natural resources in First Nations' traditional territories. (Coon Come 2003.)

Officials in the federal Department of Finance were relieved to keep off-reserve Indian income as a tax base. Most Aboriginal leaders, however, probably agreed with Coon Come: the reversal was a battle lost within a set of alien institutions in which they had historically suffered many more losses than victories.

Those who came to the SFU lecture that spring evening in 2002 could not agree, either on specific questions (should Benoît pay taxes?) or on general questions of treaty rights and obligations of citizenship. With hindsight, it is obvious that the 2002 provincial referendum was a dialogue of the deaf. On the other hand, for Canadians who are not immersed in such debates, the exchange in the halls of academe helps to illustrate the gulf between Aboriginal and non-Aboriginal perceptions of what is and what should be, and why Aboriginal policy is the most intractable conundrum the country now faces.

2 *"It Was Forced Feeding from the Start"*

In Canada's three Prairie provinces in 2000, Aboriginals in their prime earning years (ages 25 to 44) living on-reserve had median incomes just two-fifths of those of non-Aboriginals. Across Canada, Aboriginal education levels are lower, their life expectancy shorter. Prison incarceration rates, too, are much higher for Aboriginals — in Saskatchewan between 1999 and 2004, 57 percent of those who experienced at least one period of incarceration or probation were Aboriginal (Canada 2005c), an overrepresentation by a factor of four relative to the Aboriginal share of the provincial population.

Why are Aboriginals so consistently and significantly less well off than other Canadians? There are no simple answers.

In the nineteenth century, many answers were racist. Aboriginals were collectively and individually deemed incapable of mastering life in an industrial society — an inferiority, many argued, that was biologically rooted. Illustrative of attitudes in Canada in the years immediately following Confederation is the 1876 Annual Report of the Department of the Interior, which concluded:

> Our Indian legislation generally rests on the principle that the Aborigines are to be kept in a condition of tutelage and treated as

wards or children of the state....It is clearly our wisdom and our duty, through education and other means, to prepare him for a higher civilization by encouraging him to assume the privileges and responsibilities of full citizenship. (Quoted in Canada 1996, 14.)

This passage is a fair indication of much Victorian thinking, in Canada and throughout the British Empire. It was paternalist: Aboriginals as "wards or children of the state." And it displayed British imperial assumptions. Industrial civilization — with British institutions at the apex — were superior to anything that indigenous populations, from the Northwest Frontier of India to the Northwest Territories of Canada, had produced. In their defence, the officials who wrote the report avoided ugly theories of biological determinism. The Aboriginal was not biologically inferior, to be treated as a slave; rather, through education, it was possible to "prepare him for a higher civilization."

In the century after Confederation, senior officials in Ottawa were motivated by ideas best described as "pessimistic anthropology."[1] Aboriginal cultures were well adapted for traditional hunting, trapping, and fishing, but not to be part of a modern industrial society. Aboriginal norms about sharing the catch among all families, for example, were conducive to the band's survival when the success of the hunt depended on many random events, and when man-made investment in hunting tools, fishing weirs, and so on was minor. Applying the white man's norms of private property — let him who caught the catch keep all of it — would have led to prosperity for some, famine for others. The band fared better under a regime of communal property rights. The reward for good hunters lay in the power and influence they exercised in band affairs.

For anthropologists, the greatest transition in human civilization is that between hunting-trapping-fishing and sedentary agriculture. In general, the adoption of agricultural techniques permits dramatic increases in human productivity. The subsequent transition from agriculture to industry is also important, but culturally less traumatic. Agricultural yields vary with random events such

---

1 For an introduction to this concept, see Flanagan (2000, esp. chap 3).

as drought, but relative to hunting, rewards are more closely linked to individual effort — in cultivating crops, enhancing the land, and caring for domestic animals. Since successful agriculture requires long periods of time over which to evaluate the effort expended, an efficient culture should reward those who display due diligence. A regime of communal property rights does not do that. Instead, agricultural societies require norms and institutions that enable farmers to capture the rewards of their effort. The institution of private property is just, argued the liberal philosopher John Locke, because God intended man to own the fruits of his labour.[2]

To anyone versed in this anthropological tradition, hunting societies inevitably would yield in time to the superior economic productivity of settled agricultural and industrial society. Aboriginals thus had no choice but to abandon their economic and cultural traditions and adopt those of European settlers. Admittedly, this would entail cultural loss, psychological distress, and disruption of extended family links; accordingly, Ottawa had an obligation to aid in this transition.

---

2 Modern anthropologists acknowledge a more complex relationship than the simple dichotomy between, on the one hand, societies based on hunting-trapping-fishing and communal property regimes and, on the other, societies that combine settled agriculture and private property regimes. As Dr. Ulrike Radermacher of the University of British Columbia explained to me in a private communication,

> The linear thinking about human development — first hunter-gatherers, then agriculturists — is becoming out of date. It implies that hunters and gatherers are more primitive than agriculturists. For North America, that doesn't hold true: hunters and gatherers were able to develop intriguing social and political structures....For example, the First Nations on the coast of [British Columbia] had a hugely complex social system that included slaves, commoners, and nobles. The people in the Interior had a more egalitarian system, yet had gardens, planned burning, and tending of wild root growing areas.... There may have been parallel developments — people had complex economic structures in either society.

In privileged settings, a hunting society might generate high levels of productivity, become sedentary, develop hierarchies of status, and establish some private property norms. And in agricultural societies, the exercise of private property rights is frequently constrained by communal norms.

Among those responsible for Ottawa's Aboriginal policy in the early twentieth century was Duncan Campbell Scott, deputy superintendent general of Indian Affairs from 1913 to 1932. In recent years, he has been demonized as an agent of assimilation. The charge is unfair. Those who make it are applying current sensibilities to a different age. For his time and place, Scott was among the most sensitive to the distress that contact with Europeans was producing in Aboriginal communities. In addition to his official duties, he was a respected member of the group known as the Confederation Poets. More eloquent than his bureaucratic prose is his poetry. In the first part of "The Forsaken" (1905), Scott gives homage to a young Chippewa woman, who alone,

> With her sick baby
> Crouched in the last hours
> Of a great storm.
> Frozen and hungry,
> She fished through the ice
> With a line of the twisted
> Bark of the cedar,
> And a rabbit-bone hook
> Polished and barbed.

She caught nothing until

> She took of her own flesh
> Baited the fish-hook,
> Drew in a gray-trout,
> Drew in his fellows,
> Heaped them beside her.

In the second part of the poem, Scott turns to the grandchildren who abandon their grandmother and her ways:

> Years and years after,
> When she was old and withered,
> When her son was an old man
> And his children filled with vigour,
> They came in their northern tour on the verge of winter,

To an island in a lonely lake.
There one night they camped, and on the morrow
Gathered their kettles and birch-bark
Their rabbit-skin robes and their mink-traps,
Launched their canoes and slunk away through the islands,
Left her alone forever,
Without a word of farewell,
Because she was old and useless,
Like a paddle broken and warped,
Or a pole that was splintered.

The old woman prepares herself for death. She survives until the eve of the third day:

Then all light was gathered up by the hand of God and hid in His
    breast,
Then there was born a silence deeper than silence,
Then she had rest.

The idea of cultural loss and the need to accept different ways of living was not restricted to non-Aboriginal observers; Aboriginal leaders expressed similar pessimism. In a 1970 essay, Chief Dan George eloquently summarizes ideas not inherently different from those of Scott:

I was born a thousand years ago...born in a culture of bows and arrows. But within the span of half a lifetime, I was flung across the ages to the culture of the atom bomb....

I was born when people loved all nature and spoke to it as though it had a soul.

And then the people came...more and more people came...like a crushing...wave they came...hurling the years aside!...and suddenly I found myself a young man in the midst of the twentieth century.

I think it was the suddenness of it all that hurt us so. We did not have time to adjust to the startling upheaval around us. We seemed to have lost what we had without a replacement for it. We did not have time to take our 20th century progress and eat it little by little and digest it. It was forced feeding from the start and our stomachs turned sick and we vomited. (George 1970, 184–85.)

The Limits of
Pessimistic Anthropology

In the 1960s, Canada adopted new social programs, many inspired by European precedents. Saskatchewan's introduction of universal medical insurance, subsequently adopted by the nine other provinces; the expansion of postsecondary education in all the provinces, a reform pursued most enthusiastically in Quebec; Ottawa's introduction of a universal occupational pension; and federal-provincial cost sharing for social assistance are just a few of the major innovations that took place during that decade.

Aboriginal policy, too, came under increased scrutiny, via two major reviews. New policy did emerge. It was not, however, what either review advocated.

The Hawthorn Report

The first review was the Hawthorn Report (Canada 1966–67), named for its director, a prominent anthropologist. Harry Hawthorn subscribed to the pessimistic tradition of his discipline inasmuch as he envisioned most Aboriginals aspiring to industrial levels of income, something realizable only if the majority abandoned communal ways and participated in gainful employment in the Canadian industrial economy. Most Aboriginals would, he predicted, ultimately migrate to cities as had members of other communities that had originally settled in rural Canada.

Hawthorn broke with conventional wisdom, however, by insisting on diversity among Aboriginals and on the survival of reserves into an indefinite future. While many Aboriginals would become urban, some would not. For those who wanted to lead a rural, communal lifestyle, reserves would continue to be home. And for those who stayed on-reserve, band councils ought to be able to provide schools and other municipal services of reasonable quality:

To many Indians the maintenance of a separate culture is important; to others it does not matter, and many of the young in
particular would prefer to see the past transferred to the pages of
histories and ethnographies rather than have it continue into the
present. But those who cherish the language, the religion, the
special relationships of kin and association, the exchanges of
goods, support and obligation, that mark some Indian communities today should have their right to these affirmed by any program of government rather than diminished. (Canada 1966–67, 10.)

In the spirit of the 1960s, Hawthorn favoured generous social
programs. "[I]ncreasing the scope for decision by Indians" was the
goal. In particular, his report stressed the importance of better
education. Hawthorn acknowledged that better education would
encourage many to choose to live off-reserve, but assimilation was
not the goal. If they wanted their cultural identity to survive, it
would. The choice was "up to the Indian":

The research group consider it is important that cultural autonomy
not be directly lessened by any proffered political, educational or
economic changes. It is equally important that individuals be given
the capacity to make choices which include the decision to take
jobs away from reserves, play a part in politics, and move and
reside where they wish. The whole direction of the Report argues
towards increasing the scope for decision by Indians and this
includes a decision either to reside in separate cultural communities or to leave them temporarily or permanently.

Consequently the research on which the Report is based was
not directed towards finding ways in which Indians might be
assimilated, or integrated into the Canadian society without their
wish to do so, and without leaving traces of their particular and
special cultural identities. Nevertheless, it is our opinion that the
retention of these identities is up to the Indian. No official and
perhaps no outside agency at all can do that task for them.
Whether or not, and to what extent, Indians remain culturally
separate depends on what it is worth to them. And it is obvious
that equal services of all kinds should be offered and as high a

standard of schooling as for other children be given to every Indian child unless he is to be deprived of a choice. (Ibid.)

Hawthorn summarized his recommendations with the phrase "citizens plus": Registered Indians were Canadian citizens but, as the first to inhabit this territory, they enjoyed certain additional rights. Political scientist Alan Cairns, himself a researcher for the Hawthorn Report, resurrected the phrase for the title of his 2000 book on Aboriginal policy. As Cairns makes clear, Hawthorn's break with anthropological pessimism was modest relative to recent reports:

Although the [Hawthorn] Report strongly supported giving the maximum decision-making power to Indian communities, their small size and limited resources precluded the optimistic assessments that characterized the academic and political support for Indian nationhood in the 1980s and 1990s. (Cairns 2000, 163.)

Hawthorn's ideal reserves were, Cairns summarized, "villages, not nations" (162).

The 1969 White Paper

The second review was a federal White Paper, presented to Parliament in 1969 by Jean Chrétien, at the time minister of Indian Affairs and Northern Development in Pierre Trudeau's first government. Although much of Trudeau's motivation to enter federal politics was to do battle with Quebec nationalists, he nonetheless devoted considerable energy to Aboriginal policy during his first year as prime minister.

Trudeau subscribed to the ideal of citizens as individuals, bearing equal rights and obligations regardless of differences in province of residence, of language spoken, or — in this case — of racial origin. As politician, he compromised; as intellectual, he consistently displayed a French republican hostility for the British imperial tradition of accommodating group cultural differences. An example of the link Trudeau made between Quebecers and Aboriginals is a passage from a mid-1960s' polemic. In a section entitled "the wig-wam complex," he compares Quebec separatists to "kings and sorcerers" of an Indian tribe:

> The truth is that the separatist counter-revolution is the work of a powerless petit bourgeois minority afraid of being left behind by the twentieth-century revolution. Rather than carving themselves out a place in it by ability, they want to make the whole tribe return to the wigwams by declaring its independence...inside the tribe the counter-revolutionaries will be kings and sorcerers. (Trudeau 1964, 211.)

Starting with the *Quebec Act* of 1774 and continuing through to the *British North America Act* of 1867, the British had, with the exception of the 1840 *Act of Union*, afforded a special status to francophone colonists. Trudeau was ambivalent about the exceptionalism afforded on cultural grounds to different groups within Canada. If exceptionalism had fostered a wigwam complex among Quebecers, the more formal special status awarded by the *Indian Act* had been far more damaging. To Trudeau, the policy implication for both Quebecers and Indians was self-evident: eliminate special status in favour of a formal equality among all Canadians as individuals bearing equal rights and obligations.

The White Paper accordingly proposed the abolition of the *Indian Act* and the phasing out of reserves in favour of the complete integration of Aboriginals into Canadian society. The problem with past Aboriginal policy was to have accommodated traditional ways. Eliminating reserves would eliminate the crutch Aboriginals leaned on as they clung to doomed institutions.

In a speech delivered shortly after the White Paper was tabled, Trudeau summarized his rationale:

> We can go on treating the Indians as having a special status. We can go on adding bricks of discrimination around the ghetto in

which they live and at the same time perhaps helping them pre-serve certain cultural traits and certain ancestral rights. Or we can say you're at a crossroads — the time is now to decide whether the Indians will be a race apart in Canada or whether it will be Canadians of full status....It's inconceivable, I think, that in a given society one section of the society have a treaty with the other section of the society. We must all be equal under the laws and we must not sign treaties amongst ourselves....What can we do to redeem the past? I can only say as President Kennedy said when he was asked what he could do to compensate the injustices that the Negroes had received in American society: "We will be just in our time." This is all we can do. We must be just today. (Quoted in Ponting and Gibbins 1980, 27–28.)

For advocates of the White Paper — and the tradition of pessimistic anthropology of which the paper marked the logical end point — its Achilles' heel was the absence of any sizable group of well-integrated and economically successful Aboriginals. A century may not seem long to anthropologists whose studies rove millennia, but it is a very long time for a political policy to survive intact, particularly one that had yielded meagre results. Where were the successful Aboriginals willing to endorse Trudeau's argument?

Some had successfully integrated, but the great majority of Registered Indians lived at the margins of Canadian society, on-reserve and in dire poverty. Education policies were failing. Resi-dential schools, often far from parents' reserves, had created generations of unhappy, poorly educated children and, in some cases, victims of sexual and physical abuse. By the 1960s, public health authorities had contained many of the communicable dis-eases European settlers had introduced, but life expectancy was still 12 years less for Indians than for other Canadians. Rampant distress among Aboriginal families — in the form of alcoholism, family abuse, and so on — led social workers in the 1960s to resort to the large-scale apprehension of children. During that decade, one Indian child in six was, at any time, quite literally a "ward or child of the state."

From Pessimism to Optimism

A feature of the times in which the White Paper appeared was the ideology of national liberation. How could European nations, having embarked on two barbaric world wars, legitimately claim to govern those living in distant colonies? They could not. Henceforth, the principle underlying international relations would be that all communities able to define themselves as nations have the right to exercise self-government. European empires withered and died. In colony after colony, the Union Jack, the French tricolour, and other emblems of empire were replaced with flags of new design. It was a time of optimism. The leaders of these new countries spoke the language of nationalism to unite their populations around agendas of self-rule and economic development.

Some variants of Third World nationalism extolled traditional cultures while acknowledging Europe's contribution to understanding the institutional prerequisites for economic development: adequate means to protect commercial contracts, a reasonably competent public administration able among other things to organize universal primary education, and reasonably free international trade. An icon in this tradition was Kemal Attatürk. As the Ottoman Empire collapsed at the end of World War I, he prevented the victorious Allies from dismembering Turkey, and his authoritarian regime set about modernizing the country.

More radical Third World nationalists took inspiration from prevailing socialist doctrines, combining cultural affirmation with state ownership of assets and centralized planning. Egyptian leader Gamal Abdel Nasser's pan-Arabism can serve as an example. Whether moderate or radical, however, no Third World nationalists had much good to say about the departed European imperialists.

Within the capitalist First, communist Second, and ex-colonial Third Worlds existed a small Fourth World: indigenous minorities whose condition remained unchanged by the crumbling of European empires. These were tribal people dependent, not on farming, like most ex-colonial populations, but on hunting, fishing, and trapping. To the Maoris of New Zealand, the tribal people of

Burma and northeastern India, the indigenous populations of the Western Hemisphere, the peoples ringing the Arctic Ocean, and many others, the end of European imperialism meant little. Although the Fourth World's formally educated elites were few in number, they nevertheless asserted their own cultural identities while borrowing the ideas of the Third World's elites about nationhood and self-rule.

In retrospect, given the spirit of the time, it is not surprising that Aboriginal leaders in Canada largely ignored the Hawthorn Report's vision of pragmatic compromises with industrial society. The White Paper, however, was anathema. In a rebuttal dubbed the "Red Paper," the White Paper's most articulate critic, Harold Cardinal — then the young president of the Indian Association of Alberta — demanded the Canadian government honour both the letter and spirit of past treaties:

> [C]ertain promises were made to our people; some of these are contained in the text of the treaties, some in the negotiations, and some in the memories of our people. Our basic view is that all these promises are part of the treaties and must be honoured....The Indian people see the treaties as the basis of all their rights and status. If the Government expects the co-operation of Indians in any new policy, it must accept the Indian point of view on treaties. (Quoted in Allard 2002, 122.)

Since Cardinal's words, an Aboriginal cultural renaissance has come to pass across North America. Academics, lawyers, and government officials, both Aboriginal and non-Aboriginal, have filled library shelves to overflowing with books, reports, legal decisions, and articles in learned journals. Aboriginals have written highly acclaimed novels, plays, and short stories bearing on the Aboriginal condition. Aboriginal music and visual arts have enjoyed wide public attention.

A precedent to this cultural affirmation is the Harlem Renaissance, the flourishing of black cultural expression in the United States in the years following World War I. Much contemporary black writing was infused with anger at America's history of slavery and racial discrimination. So, too, is that of present-day Aboriginals. The 2003 Massey Lecture, by literary scholar and author Thomas King, is an extended indictment of the treatment of Aboriginals in North American literature and life (King 2003).

The Royal Commission on Aboriginal Peoples

If Trudeau's White Paper marked the limit of the policy pendulum's swing toward cultural assimilation, the report of the Royal Commission on Aboriginal Peoples (RCAP) might well come to be seen as the limit of the swing toward Aboriginal nationalism and what I call "optimistic anthropology." In RCAP's vision, the ideal relationship between Aboriginals and non-Aboriginals entailed virtually no shared rights or obligations. Its report prominently uses the image of the two-row wampum, a belt commemorating a 1613 treaty between the Mohawk and the Dutch:

> There are two rows of purple, and those two rows represent the spirit of our ancestors. Three beads of wampum separating the two purple rows symbolize peace, friendship and respect. The two rows of purple are two vessels traveling down the same river together. One, a birch bark canoe, is for the Indian people, their laws, their customs, and their ways. The other, a ship, is for the white people and their laws, their customs and their ways. We shall each travel the river together, side by side, but in our own boat. Neither of us will try to steer the other's vessel. (Canada 1996, 10.)

At the risk of oversimplification, let me comment briefly on three of the RCAP report's themes, which are also present, in embryo, in Harold Cardinal's Red Paper: the repudiation of the liberal notion of Aboriginals as individuals like everyone else; the use of policy to enhance the parallel powers and financial resources of reserve-based governments, and the adoption of an "optimistic anthropology" that promotes and values Aboriginals' distinctiveness.

"To Be Just in Our Time" Is Not Enough

In the liberal ideal, Indians are individuals essentially like other Canadians and accordingly should enjoy the same rights and obligations as other Canadians do. For RCAP, however, the Trudeau White Paper's refrain, "to be just in our time," was not enough. Historical wrongs — among them the failure to honour treaties and the abuse of children in residential schools — had damaged Aboriginals across the generations and required redress. Redress should be extensive and take many forms, including land transfers to Indian bands, cash transfers to band councils, tax exemptions for Indians, and the establishment and funding of Aboriginal-run health, social, and education agencies for off-reserve Aboriginals who did not want to frequent agencies serving non-Aboriginals.

RCAP's repudiation of the liberal ideal would have meant little had it been shared only among Aboriginal elites. However, sometime between the death of the 1969 White Paper as viable policy and the entrenchment of Aboriginal rights in the 1982 Constitution, Canada's non-Aboriginal governing elites had abandoned the precepts of pessimistic anthropology and the accompanying goal of integration. In their place had come "white guilt" over past wrongs and acceptance of the Aboriginal case for redress. Shelby Steele, assessing the abandonment since the 1960s of the liberal ideal in the roughly analogous case of relations between blacks and whites in the United States, writes of "two great, immutable forces" that have driven US attitudes and policies:

> The first has been white racism, and the second has been white guilt. The civil-rights movement was the dividing line between the two...the great achievement of the civil-rights movement was that its relentless oral witness finally defeated the legitimacy of racism as propriety — a principle of social organization, manners, and customs that defines decency itself....Today, thanks to the civil-rights movement, white guilt is propriety — an utterly invisible code that defines decency in our culture. (2002, 39.)

The Privileged Role of Treaties

Another of RCAP's themes is its emphasis on the use of policy to advance "parallelism": the enhancing of the powers and financial resources of reserve-based governments in order to reduce Aboriginal participation in and reliance on non-Aboriginal government programs.

This theme runs through most Aboriginal political demands over the past three decades. The primary means to realize parallelism are treaties between the governments of "First Nations" and those of non-Aboriginals. The latter, so the argument goes, represent the nation of settlers. What is required, say Aboriginals, is generous interpretation of nineteenth-century treaties and negotiation of new treaties covering Aboriginals not subject to historical treaties, as in the case of those in British Columbia. As Harold Cardinal had said, to re-establish a measure of trust in the relationship between the races, non-Aboriginals "must accept the Indian point of view on treaties." The 1996 Royal Commission report agreed:

> We propose that the treaty relationship be restored and used from now on as the basis of the partnership between Aboriginal and non-Aboriginal people in Canada.....We recommend that Canadian governments:
>
> - honour the provisions of existing treaties as recorded in treaty text and supplemented by oral evidence;
> - interpret the terms of each treaty in a broad and liberal way, in keeping with the spirit and intent of the agreements reached;
> - act as protectors of Aboriginal interests, not adversaries, and reconcile the interests of society as a whole with the terms of the treaties;
> - recognize that First Nations did not consent to loss of title to their lands or to extinguish all rights to their lands when they signed treaties — a more reasonable interpretation is that they consented to share and co-manage lands and resources;
> - recognize that by entering into treaties with Aboriginal peoples, the Crown of Canada acknowledged their inherent right of self-government, their right to control their own affairs, and their right to enter into intergovernmental arrangements with other nations. (Canada 1996, 48, 50–51.)

Optimistic Anthropology

Whatever their differences, sober analysts of the Aboriginal condition from Duncan Campbell Scott to Chief Dan George and Harry Hawthorn had concluded that most Aboriginals ultimately would want to integrate into industrial society. Over the past three decades, Aboriginal nationalism has sought to refute that conclusion. Now holding sway is a tradition of "optimistic anthropology." Culture matters as much for current advocates of Aboriginal nationalism as it did for those writing about Aboriginals in the nineteenth century. Earlier writers found Aboriginal culture to be dysfunctional for life in modern society; now, many insist that it is indispensable. Aboriginals allegedly cannot thrive as assimilated individuals; they can thrive *only* if Aboriginal governments thrive as vehicles able to promote Aboriginal cultures.

Thus, a third theme running through the RCAP report is an optimistic view of anthropology, well summarized in the following passages:

> Assimilation policies have done great damage, leaving a legacy of brokenness affecting Aboriginal individuals, families and communities. The damage has been equally serious to the spirit of Canada — the spirit of generosity and mutual accommodation in which Canadians take pride.
>
> Yet the damage is not beyond repair. The key is to reverse the assumptions of assimilation that still shape and constrain Aboriginal life chances — despite some worthy reforms in the administration of Aboriginal affairs.
>
> To bring about this fundamental change, Canadians need to understand that *Aboriginal peoples are nations* [emphasis in original]. That is, they are political and cultural groups with values and lifeways distinct from those of other Canadians. They lived as nations — highly centralized, loosely federated, or small and clan-based — for thousands of years before the arrival of Europeans. As nations, they forged trade and military alliances among themselves and with the new arrivals. To this day, Aboriginal people's sense of confidence and well-being remains tied to the strength of their nations. Only as members of restored nations can they reach their potential in the twenty-first century. (Canada 1996, x–xi.)

In short, public policy must rehabilitate Aboriginal institutions, restore to them the authority they exercised before the white settlers came. Indeed, relative to expectations at the time of the 1969 White Paper, Aboriginal leaders have already realized a good deal of the agenda of optimistic anthropology. Annual federal expenditures on Aboriginals, to take one indicator, have grown from less than $500 million in 1969 to $9 billion today, an amount approaching that of the equalization payments Ottawa sends to "have-not" provinces.

Conclusion

In Duncan Campbell Scott's poetic vision, the Aboriginal future entails an inevitable abandonment of old ways. The ways of the grandmother were worthy, but times had changed:

> [Her grandsons] launched their canoes and slunk away through
>   the islands,
> Left her alone forever,
> Without a word of farewell,
> Because she was old and useless,
> Like a paddle broken and warped,
> Or a pole that was splintered.

In RCAP's vision, by contrast, "Aboriginal people's sense of confidence and well-being remains tied to the strength of their nations. Only as members of restored nations can they reach their potential in the twenty-first century."

This transition from pessimistic to optimistic anthropology is an extraordinary — in my view, excessive — swing of the intellectual and policy pendulum. The truth, to the extent one can divine it, is at neither extreme. If Scott is guilty of a paternalistic assessment of those whom he supervised, RCAP's commissioners are guilty of romanticism about the potential of small reserve communities to contain the expectations of modern Aboriginals.

As they should, citizens of modern democracies usually judge their governments by actual performance, as opposed to first principles. In particular, they judge based on the three key criteria of education outcomes, health outcomes, and average income levels. These criteria are obviously interwoven: better-educated populations tend to be healthier and better able to get well-paying jobs.

Prior to the past three decades, the level of government primarily responsible for Aboriginal policy was unambiguously federal. Over the past 30 years, Ottawa has transferred funds and responsibility for most on-reserve services to band governments, which have assumed a much greater significance in the lives of on-reserve Aboriginals. But over these decades, Aboriginals have increasingly chosen to live off-reserve and in cities, where they receive services from provincial governments, which, like band governments, have assumed a new significance for the typical Aboriginal.

Rather than assess, in abstract, future potential swings of the pendulum between assimilation and parallelism in Ottawa's overall Aboriginal strategy, it is more useful to examine how governments — band-based, provincial, and federal — are actually performing. That is the task of the next two chapters. As preliminary, the Appendix to this chapter answers the demographic questions: who is an Aboriginal? where do Aboriginals live? how many are on-reserve, off-reserve, rural or urban, and in which provinces?

Appendix:
Defining and Counting the
Aboriginal Population

There is no single correct definition of the Aboriginal population
— different definitions are appropriate in different contexts. The
Census of Canada, from which the definitions below are taken,
provides data based on ethnic ancestry or origin, on Aboriginal
identity, on Registered Indian status, and on band membership. The
most frequently used definition is based on self-defined identity.
Unless otherwise specified, the reader can assume the Aboriginal
data discussed in this study have been prepared on an identity
basis. Table A2.1 presents 2001 population figures for each of the
census definitions.

Aboriginal ancestry/origin refers to those persons who reported
at least one Aboriginal origin (North American Indian, Métis, or Inuit)
when asked in the census about the ethnic or cultural group(s) to
which the respondent's ancestors belonged. Those reporting Aboriginal ancestry may or may not identify with this heritage.

Aboriginal identity refers to those persons who reported in the
census as identifying with at least one Aboriginal group (North
American Indian, Métis, or Inuit). A person identifying as Aboriginal, however, does not necessarily have Aboriginal ancestry. Also
included in this definition are individuals who, while not reporting
an Aboriginal identity, did report themselves as a Registered or Treaty
Indian and/or as having a band membership.

Registered, Status, or Treaty Indian refers to those who reported
in the census that they were registered as Indians under the *Indian
Act*. The registry, maintained independently of the census by the
Department of Indian Affairs, consists of persons who can prove
descent from a band that signed a treaty. Since the initial enumeration of band members was often imperfect, the distinction between
Indian-identity Aboriginals who are and are not registered is somewhat arbitrary. Indeed, the distinction between Registered Indians
and those who define themselves as Métis is also somewhat arbitrary.
The term "Treaty Indian" is widely used in the Prairie provinces.

Table A2.1: *The Aboriginal Population by Census Definition, 2001*

Census Definition		Number
Aboriginal origin		1,319,900
Aboriginal identity		976,300
of which,		
Indian identity	608,900	
Métis identity	292,300	
Inuit identity	45,100	
Other/mixed identity	30,100	
Registered Indian		
Census count		558,175
Indian Affairs count		690,100[a]
Band membership		554,860

[a] Total number of Registered Indians in 2001, as reported by the Department of Indian Affairs (Canada 2004b, 4).

Source: Canada 2003b.

One reason for the difference between these counts is incomplete on-reserve census enumeration.

Member of an Indian Band refers to those persons who reported being a member of an Indian band.

"First Nations." Over the past two decades, the term "First Nations" has been extensively used to describe Indian bands and tribal groupings. I have generally avoided use of the term because of the ambiguity inherent in the meaning of the word "nation." It may refer to a group of people sharing a particular culture; alternatively, it may refer to a group of people, with no shared cultural features, living under a particular political regime. On occasion, "First Nations" is intended to embrace the first meaning. At other times, its use implies acceptance of a political agenda in which the "First Nations" share no significant cultural features with other "nations" within Canada, and consequently share few rights and obligations of citizenship with other Canadians. Much as the use of "Quebec nation" may frustrate clear thinking about the culture and

Table A2.2: *Aboriginal Identity Population,*
by Province/Territory and in Selected Cities, 2001

	Population		Aboriginal Share of Jurisdiction's Population	
	Province/ Territory	City	Province/ Territory	City
	(number)		*(percent)*	
Newfoundland and Labrador	18,780		3.7	
Prince Edward Island	1,345		1.0	
Nova Scotia	17,015		1.9	
New Brunswick	16,990		2.3	
Quebec	79,400		1.1	
Montreal		11,085		0.3
Ontario	188,315		1.7	
Toronto		20,300		0.4
Ottawa-Hull		13,485		1.3
Manitoba	150,040		13.4	
Winnipeg		55,755		8.4
Saskatchewan	130,190		13.3	
Saskatoon		20,275		9.1
Regina		15,685		8.3
Prince Albert		11,640		29.2
Alberta	156,220		5.3	
Edmonton		40,930		4.4
Calgary		21,915		2.3
British Columbia	170,025		4.4	
Vancouver		36,860		1.9
Yukon Territory	6,540		22.8	
Northwest Territories	18,725		50.1	
Nunavut	22,720		85.0	
Canada	976,310		3.3	

Source: Canada 2003b.

politics of Quebecers, so may the use of "First Nations" impede rational discussion of Aboriginal issues.

The quick snapshot of the Aboriginal population taken by the 2001 Census reveals that it is distributed unevenly across Canada: of every 20 Aboriginals, 12 live in one of the four western provinces, 4 live in Ontario, 2 in Quebec, 1 in the Atlantic region, and 1 in the territories (see Table A2.2). The Aboriginal population is also relatively young. Since fertility is higher for Aboriginal women than for other Canadian women, the median age of Aboriginals is lower: 24.7 years compared with 37.7 years for non-Aboriginals. In Manitoba and Saskatchewan, one person in seven is Aboriginal, as is one child in four under the age of 15.

The snapshot also reveals that the Aboriginal population is becoming more urban: a quarter of all Aboriginals now live in the ten cities listed in Table A2.2. In 2001, 31 percent — less than a third — of the Aboriginal identity population lived on-reserve; 20 percent lived in a rural, off-reserve community; and 49 percent lived in a city. Among those identifying as Indian, as opposed to Métis or Inuit, 47 percent — slightly fewer than half — lived on-reserve. The off-reserve share of the Registered Indian population doubled between the 1960s and 1990s. The 2001 Census reports, however, a small net migration back to reserves over the past decade. Aboriginal residential mobility nevertheless remains high — roughly twice that for non-Aboriginals — and many Aboriginals move back and forth between reserve and off-reserve communities.

3 *Why the Gap in Health Outcomes?*

Since 1899, when Sifton's commissioners came west to negotiate what is now known as Treaty 8, a massive migration of Aboriginals has taken place. Two in three of the Aboriginal population no longer live on-reserve, and half of all Aboriginals now live in cities. A century ago, the health of Aboriginals — for example, their high incidence of tuberculosis — was a shameful blot on the reputation of a young Dominion concerned about its citizens' well-being. Have migration and the many other changes in Aboriginal conditions over the twentieth century caused the health outcomes of Aboriginals to converge with those of non-Aboriginals? The answer is a qualified yes. Much of that convergence, however, took place only in the last quarter of the century, and the rate of convergence seemingly slowed in the 1990s.

As recently as 1975, life expectancy at birth for Registered Indians was 11 years shorter than for all Canadians and roughly the same as it then was in China. The Aboriginal infant-mortality rate was more than twice as high as the rate for other Canadians and close to the rate then prevailing in the Soviet Union.[1] Since the mid-1970s, most

---

1 Life expectancy at birth is a statistic that captures the effect of all factors — such as the quality of available health services, nutrition, mental illness,...

countries have managed to both lower infant mortality and raise life expectancy, and so have Canada's Aboriginals.[2] Life-expectancy and infant-mortality rates among Registered Indians are now at levels prevailing in the best-organized eastern European health systems, such as those of Poland and Slovakia,[3] while the life-expectancy gap between Indians and other Canadians has narrowed to six years (see Figure 3.1).[4]

Some credit for the convergence of Aboriginal and non-Aboriginal health outcomes must go to rising levels of education and income among Aboriginals, since people with more education and higher incomes enjoy, on average, better health. Improved access to health services has also helped close the gap — indeed, by 2002, the Romanow Commission on health care (Canada 2002a) reported evidence that health care use was higher among some Aboriginal groups than among other Canadians[5] — although access to services remains inadequate in some isolated communities.

Note 1 - cont'd.

...health-damaging lifestyles, and environmental risks — that bear on mortality. Infant mortality rates for any year are measured as deaths among infants under age 1 relative to the number of live births.

2   Russia is an unfortunate exception: its infant-mortality rate has declined, but so too has life expectancy.

3   The international comparisons are drawn from United Nations (2004).

4   Many of the statistics in this chapter refer to the Registered Indian population — individuals on the registry maintained by the federal Department of Indian Affairs. Health statistics are more readily available for this group than for more broadly defined groups of Aboriginals. Among all groups, Aboriginal and non-Aboriginal, better health outcomes (as measured by longer life expectancy, lower incidence of particular illnesses, better self-reported health status, and so on) are usually positively correlated with higher education and income levels (Tjepkema 2002). Since education and income levels are higher, in general, among non-Indian Aboriginals (such as Métis) than among Registered Indians, the gap between average health outcomes of Registered Indians and those of all Canadians is probably higher than those between all Aboriginals and all Canadians. Since education and income levels are higher among off-reserve Indians than among those on-reserve, the health gap may be assumed to be wider still between on-reserve Indians and other Canadians.

5   The Romanow Commission reported, for example, that average rates of visits to a physician and admissions to hospital were higher among Indians in...

Figure 3.1:   *Life-Expectancy Comparisons, Registered*
                  Indians and All Canadians, by Sex, 1975–2005

A.   *Life Expectancy at Birth*

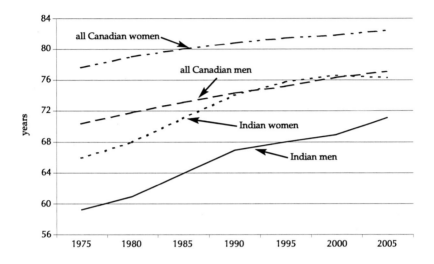

B.   *Life-Expectancy Gaps*

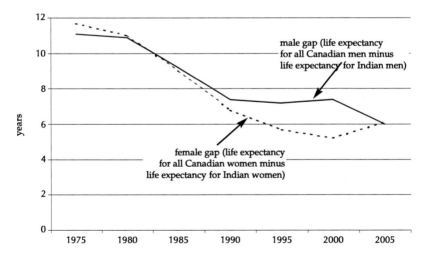

Source: Canada 2004b, 26.

As opposed to quantity, what about the *quality* of the health services Aboriginals receive? Infant mortality serves as a good proxy for overall quality, for a couple of reasons. First, although infant mortality has many causes, sick babies' lives often can be saved by the intervention of a competent health care provider. Second, sick babies have not had time to develop injurious lifestyle habits whose consequences burden the health care system. On that basis, then, Aboriginals have made much progress. As recently as 1980, the infant-mortality rate of on-reserve Indians was nearly two and a half times that of all Canadians. By 2000, the Indian infant-mortality rate had dropped to nearly the national average (see Table 3.1).

It is probably fair to conclude that most Aboriginals now have access to health services of comparable quality and quantity to those enjoyed by other Canadians. Some portion of the remaining gap may be due to the fact that Indians are more likely than other Canadians to live in rural regions, and infant-mortality rates are slightly higher for rural Canadians generally than for those living in urban areas. However, a disturbing fact remains: the life-expectancy gap between Aboriginals and non-Aboriginals has not closed but merely narrowed; moreover, the rate of convergence has slowed dramatically.[6]

Explaining the Gap

Some insight into explaining the remaining health gap between Aboriginals and non-Aboriginals can be had through statistical exercises that determine the "potential years of life lost" (PYLL)

Note 5 - cont'd.

...Manitoba than among other residents of the province. In Saskatchewan in recent years, total spending on health services by the federal and provincial governments is about twice as high per capita for Aboriginals as for other Saskatchewan residents. (Canada 2002a, 217–18.)

6   In the 15 years between 1975 and 1990, the life-expectancy gap fell by roughly four percentage points for men and five for women. In the subsequent 15 years between 1990 and 2005, the gap fell by only about one percentage point for both sexes.

Table 3.1: *Selected Health Outcomes,*
   Aboriginal and Non-Aboriginal Canadians

Vital Statistics	Indians On-Reserve	All Canadians
Infant mortality	*(deaths per 1,000 live births)*	
1980	23.7	10.4
2000	6.4	5.5
Age-specific birth rates[a]	*(live births per 1,000 women)*	
Ages 15–19	106.3	19.9
20–24	173.7	64.2
25–29	131.7	104.1
30–34	73.2	84.9
35–39	32.2	32.8
40–44	6.6	5.3
Total	23.0	11.1

Communicable Diseases	All Aboriginals	Non-Aboriginals
HIV/AIDS	*(percent)*	
Distribution of ethnically identified AIDS cases, 1979–2003[b]	3.1	96.9
Distribution of ethnically identified HIV cases, 1998-2003[c]	23.0	77.0

Non-Communicable and Chronic Conditions	Aboriginals Off-Reserve	Non-Aboriginals
Major depressive episode in past year, by income level, 2000[d]	*(percent)*	
Low income	21	13
Middle income	13	9
High income	7	6
Obesity		
Low or acceptable (BMI under 25)	45.2	54.2
Overweight (25 < BMI < 30)	32.0	31.8
Obese (BMI > 30)[e]	22.8	14.1
Alcohol abuse		
Heavy drinking[f]	26.1	16.1

Table 3.1 - continued

	Indians On-Reserve	All Canadians
Smoking	*(percent)*	
Proportion smoking (Indians, 1997; all Canadians, 2000)	62 (Inuit, 72)	23
Suicide	*(deaths per 100,000)*	
Rate (1999)	27.9	13.2

[a] Indian statistics exclude Quebec; Canadian data exclude Newfoundland and Labrador. Indian birth rates are for 1999; Canadian rates are for 1997.

[b] Between 1979 and 2003, 16,244 of 18,934 AIDS cases were identified by ethnicity.

[c] Between 1998 and 2003, 3,706 of 12,602 HIV-positive tests were identified by ethnicity.

[d] The survey posed questions to identify the presence of a cluster of symptoms associated by the Diagnostic and Statistical Manual with depression. The responses were scored and transformed into a probability of diagnosing a major depressive episode. If the probability exceeded 0.9, the respondent was deemed to have experienced a major depressive episode. See Tjepkema (2002, 4) for details on determination of income cutoffs.

[e] Body mass index (BMI) is equal to weight in kilograms divided by height in metres.

[f] Heavy drinking is defined as consuming five or more alcoholic drinks on one occasion, and doing so once a month or more.

Sources: Infant mortality, Canada 2004b, 29; age-specific birth rates, Canada 2003b, 18; HIV/AIDS, Canada 2004d; major depressive episodes, Tjepkema 2002, 7; obesity, alcohol abuse, idem, 13–16; smoking, Canada 2003a, 52; suicide rate, idem, 34.

attributable to various causes of death. For example, if everyone in a community lived to a pre-specified ripe old age, then, by construction, the PYLL for that population would be zero. That is the ideal, and obviously no community achieves it. The younger the age at which a particular cause of death strikes and the more prevalent it is, the larger is its impact on the PYLL for the population.

Health Canada conducted a PYLL exercise survey of on-reserve Indians and the general Canadian population in 1999, some results of which are summarized in Table 3.2. The most startling finding is the overwhelming importance among on-reserve Indians of the "injury" category,[7] a major component of which is suicide. Suicide is more than twice as common among on-reserve Indians than among other Canadians and in 1999 was the cause of 38 percent of on-reserve deaths of Indians ages 10 to 19 and 23 percent of deaths among Indians ages 20 to 44 (Canada 2003a, 34). Suicide accounted for roughly a quarter of the years of life lost due to injury among Indians and for more than a third of the total difference in the PYLL of Indians and non-Indians.

To go beyond describing these differences in health status and attempt to explain them is, however, an exercise fraught with uncertainty. Explanations fall into three broad categories, and deciding among them is in many cases no easy task.

Genetic Differences

The first category comprises explanations based on genetic differences. It is well established, for example, that the greater prevalence of sickle cell anaemia among Americans of African origin than among those of European origin is due to a genetic predisposition among the former to the disease. More controversially, because the evidence is generally lacking, some argue that interethnic differences in obesity rates are explicable in terms of genetic differences in metabolism.

---

7   In this category alone, the gap between on-reserve Indians and other Canadians — 3,638 PYLL per 100,000 population — exceeded the total PYLL gap between the two groups. The injury gap can exceed the total because in some other disease categories the Indian PYLL is less than that for other Canadians.

Table 3.2: *Relative Importance of Cause of Death,*
On-Reserve Indians and All Canadians, 1999

	Indians On-Reserve	All Canadians	Difference	Distribution of Difference
	(potential years of life lost per 100,000 population)			*(percent)*
Injury (including suicide)	4,909	1,271	3,638	104.5
Circulatory	900	961	–61	–1.8
Cancer	770	1,617	–847	–24.3
Perinatal	329	211	118	3.4
Congenital	293	178	115	3.3
Digestive	280	177	103	3.0
Respiratory	247	201	46	1.3
Endocrine	225	148	77	2.2
Mental	142	60	82	2.4
Nervous	137	144	–7	–0.2
Musculoskeletal	70	16	54	1.6
Genitourinary	45	39	6	0.2
Blood	10	17	–7	–0.2
Ill-defined	294	130	164	4.7
Total	8,651	5,170	3,481	100.0

Note: Causes of death are classified according to the International Classification of Diseases. See the text for a definition of potential years of life lost.

Source: Author's adaptation from Canada 2003a, 31.

Socio-Cultural Differences

Nutritionists praise Mediterranean and Japanese diets for their low share of calories derived from saturated fats, while criticizing the high level of saturated fat in the typical North American diet. Such differences have something to do with geography — olive trees grow well along the Mediterranean, but not in Kansas — but what we eat is greatly influenced by inherited culinary culture. Nutritionists are almost certainly right to insist that diet helps to explain life-expectancy differences among ethnic groups, and to that extent the cultural explanation matters. Along similar lines, there is evidence, albeit fragmentary, that the prevalence of AIDS is rising faster among Aboriginals than among non-Aboriginals (see Table 3.1), the explanation for which presumably lies in cultural differences in sexual behaviour.

Not surprisingly, the optimistic anthropology tradition has inspired researchers to expand on cultural explanations of the Aboriginal–non-Aboriginal health gap. Over the past decade many studies have appeared under the auspices of the Harvard Project on American Indian Economic Development, part of the Kennedy School of Government at Harvard University. A significant number are case studies illustrating how particular reservations have realized improvements in health outcomes.[8] The organizing thesis behind all the Project's work is that the cultural distinction between Aboriginals and other Americans requires autonomous Aboriginal institutions as the necessary precondition for Aboriginal economic and social progress (Cornell and Kalt 1998).

Closer to home, a cultural explanation for adverse Aboriginal health outcomes appears in a major study of suicide among Aboriginals in British Columbia ages 15 to 24, for whom the rate was three times that for non-Aboriginals over a five-year period in the late 1980s and early 1990s (Chandler and Lalonde 1998). The authors establish the residence of each Aboriginal suicide in one of 29 tribal councils. Then, using an index of the degree of "cultural continuity" that each tribal council exercises — based on such measures as the percentage of children attending on-reserve schools and the extent of band control of health and other services — the authors find that the higher is the tribal council's index of cultural continuity, the lower is the suicide rate within the council.

Incentives and Individual Choices

The third category of explanation assumes that differences in health outcomes across groups are primarily the result of major differences

---

8   The Harvard Project administers the "Honoring Nations" program, which acknowledges reservations that demonstrate excellent management. The list of recipients is available from Internet web site: www.ksg.harvard.edu/hpaied.

in the incentives that impinge on individuals' choices. In this category, neither genetic nor cultural differences figure centrally.

To return to the problem of suicide, it is well established that the poor and unemployed are more prone to clinical depression, itself a risk factor associated with suicide (see, for example, World Health Organization 2004). What this suggests is that the Chandler and Lalonde study of suicide among Aboriginal youth is incompletely specified in the sense that considerations of "cultural continuity" are inadequate. In addition to "cultural continuity," a more comprehensive study would assess the impact of labour market outcomes — frequent unemployment, low income, and so on. The Chandler and Lalonde study provides support for those who favour a policy of enhanced Aboriginal self-government. But what if band councils tolerate high dropout rates from school or discourage the search for employment by automatically granting social assistance? The incentives in such a situation are to remain unemployed and rely on welfare. The optimum policy to reduce suicide might be quite different from that of Chandler and Lalonde. Self-government may help, but only if the performance of Aboriginal schools improves dramatically, and welfare-to-work reforms are implemented to lower on-reserve reliance on social assistance.

The Case of Diabetes

A good way to appreciate alternate explanations for health outcomes and the implication for policy is via the case of diabetes (see Box 3.1). An ominous health trend over the past quarter-century has been the increase in the prevalence of diabetes among North Americans. Moreover, as Table 3.3 shows, that increase has been much more pronounced among Aboriginals than among the general population.[9] Health Canada's 1999 PYLL survey of on-reserve Indians inadequately captures the seriousness of diabetes as a health concern for at least two reasons. First, the still-increasing prevalence of the disease among Aboriginals means that its importance will be higher

9   See Canada 2000a; Young et al. 2000; Norris, Siggner, and Costa 2003.

Box 3.1: *Diabetes and Obesity*

Diabetes refers to a syndrome in which the blood sugar level does not stay within an acceptable range. Over time, diabetes may induce loss of vision due to destruction of the retina, and increase the risk of a coronary. Extremely high blood sugar levels induce coma and death (Florence and Yeager 1999). In early stages, symptoms may be minor, and diabetes is accordingly under-diagnosed.

Insulin, secreted by the pancreas, is the key enzyme regulating cell uptake of blood sugar. In the case of Type-I diabetes, the pancreas is defective, usually from birth. Treatment requires daily administration of insulin. Type-II diabetes arises from prolonged excess demand on the pancreas to produce insulin, resulting finally in collapse of the organ's functioning.

The causes of Type-II diabetes are less clear. Genetic propensity may be a relevant risk factor. Another is obesity. If caloric intake is high relative to caloric expenditure, the body's response is to secrete additional insulin. For many years, the only adverse effect may be obesity as the body transforms sugars into fat. Ultimately, cells begin to develop insulin resistance, and blood sugar uptake requires ever-higher insulin levels. The pancreas cannot indefinitely accommodate this ever-higher requirement. At this point, insulin levels become inadequate; diabetes symptoms become apparent, and patients require administration of insulin.

There is evidence that appropriate changes in lifestyle — increased physical activity combined with lowered caloric intake — reduce the incidence of diabetes among those at risk, and that such changes may restore appropriate pancreatic functioning (Tuomilehto et al. 2001).

---

in future PYLL exercises than in the 1999 survey. Second, diabetes is often a relevant risk factor for other illnesses that become the proximate cause of death. For example, diabetes increases the probability of a patient's suffering a heart attack or stroke.

Why is diabetes becoming more prevalent among Aboriginals? In a Statistics Canada assessment of the health of off-reserve Aboriginals, Michael Tjepkema concludes:

> It is thought that the rise of these "new" diseases, such as diabetes and cardiovascular disease, can be attributed to the rapid social,

Table 3.3: *Prevalence of Diabetes among Aboriginals On- and Off-Reserve and All Canadians, by Age Group, 2000*

Age	On-Reserve Aboriginals	Off-Reserve Aboriginals	All Canadians
	(percent)		
15–24	2.0	0.9	0.3
25–34	7.0	3.0	1.0
35–44	11.0	6.8	2.0
45–64	19.0	11.5	4.3
55–64	32.0	18.9	8.7
65+	32.0	22.2	12.7

Note: Data refer to self-reported prevalence of diabetes among the Aboriginal identity population. The on-reserve data are from the reserves participating in the *Aboriginal Peoples Survey*. They may not be representative.

Source: Norris et al. 2003.

dietary, and lifestyle changes experienced by some Aboriginal communities over this period. These health inequalities are explained, in part, by the fact that Aboriginal people have lower socio-economic status than other Canadians, a characteristic that is widely known to be associated with poor health. (2002, 1.)

Tjepkema fully understands the correlation of diabetes with proximate variables such as obesity, but his emphasis on low socio-economic status as the root cause obviously places his analysis in the socio-cultural category of explanation. It is an explanation cast in general historical terms, and it invites a skeptical question: Since the social status of Aboriginals was undoubtedly lower a quarter-century ago than it is now, and if low status is the key independent variable, why did the diabetes epidemic not manifest itself earlier?

Several epidemiologists have put forward a theory that combines genetic and socio-cultural explanations. The hypothesis is that Aboriginals may have a genetic propensity to contract diabetes when exposed to the high-carbohydrate diets characteristic of societies that have crossed the developmental stage of intensive agriculture. The ancestors of European and Asian settlers switched to such a diet many millennia ago, long before they reached North America. Aboriginals abandoned the high-protein diet of hunting-trapping-fishing societies only recently.[10]

In a 1986 study of diabetes among Registered Indians, Kue Young and his colleagues (Young et al. 1990) discovered that the prevalence of diagnosed cases was lowest in the northern territories. This they attributed to the low interaction of Aboriginals in those areas with industrial society and their maintenance of a traditional high-protein diet. In southern Canada, they found a marked gradient in diabetes prevalence, ranging from not much higher in British Columbia than in the North to a rate four times higher in Atlantic Canada. This gradient is consistent with the idea that different Aboriginal groupings possess different genetic propensities for diabetes.

If genes-plus-diet is the ultimate explanation, there is not much to be done in terms of diabetes prevention other than give advice on diet. There is, however, a third line of explanation. Researchers agree that obesity is a major factor in increasing the risk of incurring diabetes, and obesity is more prevalent among Aboriginals than among non-Aboriginals — although, of course, increasing obesity is a problem in most industrial societies. If public policies have disproportionately created incentives among Aboriginals to reduce caloric expenditure and/or increase caloric intake, then the policy emphasis obviously shifts. Changing public policy may have limited effect but the emphasis should be on undoing the perverse incentives. Consider some of the evidence on obesity trends.

Between the early 1970s and early 1990s, the proportion of obese individuals rose from 15 percent to 28 percent of the US population (Cutler, Glaeser, and Shapiro 2003, 97).[11] Holding constant any

---

10 For elaboration of the hypothesis that Aboriginals possess a "thrifty genotype" predisposing them to diabetes in the context of a North American diet, see the Health Canada report on diabetes prevalence (Canada 2000a).

11 In the public health literature, the imprecise ideas of underweight and overweight are defined in terms of body mass index (BMI). The BMI for an individual equals his or her weight in kilograms divided by the square of height in metres. A standard definition of overweight is a BMI in the range of 25 to 30; of obesity, a BMI in excess of 30.

genetically induced effects, the explanation resides in some combination of an increase in per capita caloric intake and a reduction in per capita energy expended. After looking at detailed activity surveys among thousands of individuals, Cutler and his colleagues doubt there was any overall reduction in average energy expended over the two decades. On the other hand, they estimate that average daily caloric intake increased by more than 10 percent, which, they conclude, is the probable culprit in rising rates of obesity. They go further and link caloric intake to advances in industrial techniques applied to food preparation (such as vacuum packing, improved preservatives, deep freezing, and microwaves) and to restaurants (fast-food chains). These changes lowered the cost of food preparation and, therefore, of restaurant meals. In short, falling food costs and rising incomes have induced Americans to eat more than is good for them.

Although the daily energy expended by the average American may have changed little between the 1970s and the 1990s, there was certainly a significant decline in energy expenditure between the early part of the twentieth century and the 1970s, as the share of the labour force engaged in physically arduous work, such as farm labour, fell. Moreover, technological advances have allowed appliances to be substituted for much of the domestic manual labour formerly needed to raise children and maintain a household. For Aboriginals, however, the larger change in incentives bearing on caloric energy expenditure is in the incentives to undertake work beyond domestic tasks — either in the form of paid employment for others or self-employment in traditional activities.

The great expansion of social programs by Ottawa and the provinces since the end of World War II has induced many Aboriginals to change their lifestyle, to rely increasingly on government transfer income, and to work less at arduous traditional activities. Aboriginal reliance on social assistance increased in the 1950s when publicly funded relief became available. It further increased in the early 1970s as Ottawa accepted the strategy of institutional parallelism and increased fiscal transfers to bands. For the past two decades, on-reserve welfare beneficiaries have on average exceeded

40 percent of the on-reserve population. For comparison, over the last three decades, the peak for the comparable statistic among the off-reserve (Aboriginal and non-Aboriginal) population occurred in the mid-1990s, at 10 percent; by 2001, it had fallen back to 6 percent.[12]

What Explains the Prevalence of Diabetes?

What evidence exists to support one or another of the suggested explanations — genes-plus-diet, low socio-cultural status, incentives to increase caloric intake and/or reduce caloric expenditure — for the prevalence of diabetes among Aboriginals? An important source of data is the *Aboriginal Peoples Survey* (Canada 2004a), conducted in conjunction with the 2001 Census. Using the survey, my research assistant and I derived rates of employment and diabetes prevalence in 24 discrete Aboriginal communities: those living in the ten cities with the largest Aboriginal populations, and those living both on- and off-reserve in seven other regions. Figure 3.2 plots diabetes prevalence among these 24 groups against their respective employment rates.

If genes-plus-diet explains the prevalence of diabetes among Aboriginals, and if region of residence is an adequate proxy for different genetic groups, one would expect to find two outcomes. First, one would expect the same west-to-east gradient of prevalence in 2001 as Young and his colleagues found from earlier data. Second, since off-reserve Aboriginals presumably have adopted a non-Aboriginal diet to a greater extent than have those on-reserve, the prevalence of diabetes should be higher off-reserve than on-reserve. To the extent that socio-cultural status matters and reserves are the source of Aboriginal cultural continuity and psychological well-being, the prevalence of diabetes again should be higher off-

---

12 On-reserve welfare utilization statistics since 1980 are drawn from various issues of *Basic Departmental Data*, published annually by the Department of Indian Affairs. For the most recent issue, see Canada (2004b). Other sources of data for this discussion are Canada (1980, 28) and Moscovitch and Webster (1995, 218–25). For trends in off-reserve welfare utilization, see Richards (2005).

Figure 3.2:   *Prevalence of Diabetes among Aboriginals,*
by Place of Residence and Employment Rate, 2001

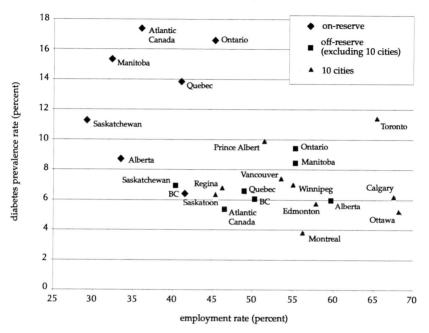

Source: Author's calculations, from 2001 Census of Canada data.

reserve. Hence, from the perspective of either the genes-plus-diet or the low-status hypothesis, one should expect diabetes to be more prevalent among off-reserve Aboriginals than among those on-reserve.

Based on simple regression analysis (see regression 1 in the Appendix to this chapter), regional variables do not explain much of the variance in diabetes prevalence. A west-to-east gradient of diabetes prevalence remains evident among on-reserve Aboriginals, but the gradient does not hold for those living off-reserve. For example, diabetes prevalence among those living on-reserve in Quebec is among the highest in the country, while among Aboriginals living in Montreal it is the lowest.

As for the conclusion that, for reasons of genes-plus-diet or low status, diabetes would be less common among on-reserve Aboriginals than among those off-reserve, the data reveal otherwise. Typical on-reserve populations experience diabetes prevalence rates nearly twice those prevailing off-reserve (regression 2). Including regional variables does not change this result. However, there is now (in regression 4) some reasonably significant evidence of a west-to-east gradient. Whatever problems off-reserve Aboriginals may experience in terms of cultural loss or diet, they are faring dramatically better in terms of avoiding diabetes.

The data also support the conclusion that those who are employed tend to experience significantly less diabetes (regression 3). If, as above, we include regional variables (regression 5), the beneficial effect of employment remains significant, but there is again evidence of a west-to-east gradient. According to this last regression, a four-percentage-point increase in a population's employment rate lowers diabetes prevalence by one percentage point. The implication is that, were it possible to raise the 37 percent average employment rate that prevails on-reserve to the 57 percent rate of urban Aboriginals, the prevalence of diabetes among on-reserve Aboriginals would fall by five percentage points — that is, by nearly half.

To repeat the caveat stated above, explaining health outcomes is fraught with uncertainty. That said, what can one conclude? There is some support from the regional variables (in regressions 1, 4, and 5) for the genes-plus-diet explanation. But this explanation is not consistent with the result that off-reserve Aboriginals fare significantly better than those on-reserve (regressions 2 and 4). The inverse relation between employment and diabetes prevalence is consistent with the thesis that policies enabling large-scale reliance on social assistance have contributed to high diabetes prevalence (regressions 3 and 5). Admittedly, these regressions attempt to explain diabetes prevalence in terms of a small number of variables, and in doing so they exclude other potentially relevant variables. They also ignore the fact that variables may be interrelated.

As I discuss in the next chapter, there is a strong link between average Aboriginal employment rates and median incomes. Higher off-reserve Aboriginal employment rates imply not only a more active lifestyle but also higher incomes, and people with higher incomes typically enjoy healthier diets. In other words, the employment and on-/off-reserve variables are, to some extent, capturing the effect of income on diabetes prevalence.

The Effect of Aboriginal Health Program Delivery

Another key factor in determining Aboriginal health outcomes is the way in which Aboriginal health programs are delivered. The federal government finances on-reserve health services — and some services to Registered Indians living off-reserve — through the First Nations and Inuit Health Branch of Health Canada. The annual budget of the branch approaches $2 billion.[13]

In the preface to a recent report, the branch offered the following vision statement: "First Nations and Inuit people will have autonomy and control of their health programs and resources within a time-frame to be determined in consultation with First Nations and Inuit people" (Canada 2002b, front matter). The branch implies, although with some qualification, that at some point there will be a complete institutional separation of health services provided to Aboriginals from those delivered to other Canadians. Is this goal appropriate?

The current reality is that Aboriginal health services are administered and financed through an unsatisfactory accretion of *ad hoc* programs. The Romanow Commission on health care refers to the funding situation as "confusing and unsatisfactory" (Canada 2002a, 217). Aboriginal bands and Health Canada organize health services under bewildering financial arrangements that preclude accountability for outcomes, even as Ottawa assumes responsibility for financing all health services for on-reserve Indians. Health Canada officials regard this as a discretionary decision flowing from the federal government's jurisdiction over Indians. Band councils typically disagree, considering Ottawa's responsibility to be a treaty obligation (ibid., 212). It is unclear what the courts would decide in

---

13 Much of this section is drawn from Richards (2002), a report prepared for the Romanow Commission on health care (Canada 2002a).

the event of litigation. To complicate matters further, most health services for Registered Indians are provided by agencies not under federal jurisdiction — in some instances, bands themselves hire health care workers for those on-reserve; in other cases, the band or Indian Affairs contracts services from the relevant province. The channels for financing these services are also convoluted: Health Canada undertakes some expenditures directly; bands undertake some using funds transferred from Health Canada; some spending comes from the provinces, which occasionally can be reimbursed by Health Canada; and some spending is undertaken by individual care providers, also with reimbursement by Health Canada. In short, no single agency is effectively responsible for spending on Aboriginal health programs, and no agency can readily redirect resources in the interest of better outcomes.

Non-insured health benefits (NIHB) are another *ad hoc* approach to Aboriginal health. Ottawa gives Registered Indians, both on- and off-reserve, insurance benefits for services — such as dental services — that provincial health insurance programs do not cover for other Canadians. Whether such generosity toward Indians (but not other Aboriginals or non-Aboriginals) is a treaty benefit or a matter of discretionary policy, in either case the status quo generates a sense of inequity among those who pay taxes but receive less generous insured health services.

Like other governments, band councils face demands to use their health budgets for purposes not directly related to health services. On-reserve unemployment and poverty make this pressure particularly acute. The result may be excessively lengthy patient hospital stays, weak accounting control of health-related travel expenses, and other problems.[14] Yet the concerns of the federal Department of Finance and the provincial finance ministries about the rapid escalation in Aboriginal health expenditures[15] come in a context

---

14 As an indication of the shaky state of accounting control, transportation accounted for 31 percent of the total of $628 million in NIHB payments in fiscal year 2001/02, the largest single component (Canada 2002b, 22).

15 Total NIHB payments grew at an average annual rate of 7 percent over fiscal years 1998/99 to 2001/02 (Canada 2002b, 20).

where administrative complexity and political sensitivities render the exercise of fiscal controls and value-for-money auditing exceedingly difficult.

Reforming Aboriginal Health Care Delivery

When the prime minister, premiers, and leaders of the major Aboriginal organizations met in Kelowna, BC, in late 2005, they broached — in unduly general terms — the problems of administering health care delivery for Aboriginals. The background paper to the meeting promised "concrete initiatives to improve delivery of and access to health services...without unnecessary duplication and creation of parallel health care systems" (Canada 2005d, 8).

It seems to me that there are four broad options for the future of Aboriginal health care delivery:

- continue with the current *ad hoc* approach;
- devolve health care delivery to bands or regional councils of local bands;
- create joint federal-provincial-Aboriginal "partnerships" (as recommended by the Romanow Commission) responsible for health services among Aboriginals who opt in; or
- transfer responsibility for delivery of on-reserve health services to provincial governments.

Continue the *Ad Hoc* Approach

Although the status quo exhibits many inadequacies, major improvements in Aboriginal access to health services have taken place over the past quarter-century. These improvements have come about as a result of good-faith endeavours by Health Canada, band councils, provincial health departments, and individual care providers. Staying the course at least would avoid the political conflict inherent in the other three options. The obvious disadvantage of maintaining the status quo is that it does nothing about its own inadequacies.

Devolve Delivery to the Bands

The option of devolving the delivery of health care services to bands would entail interpreting health benefits explicitly as a treaty obligation and transferring administrative control over the spending of funds to band councils. To avoid some of the problems with health planning undertaken by small individual bands, responsibility might be transferred to regional councils representing several bands within a geographic area. This option, in fact, reflects the recommendations of the Royal Commission on Aboriginal Peoples. It would do little to relieve the problems of the status quo, however, and might well exacerbate them.

Form Joint Partnerships

The report of the Romanow Commission on health care, in its chapter on Aboriginal health policy (Canada 2002a, 211–31), advocates consolidating federal and provincial health-related spending on Aboriginals into "Aboriginal Health Partnerships," to be managed by some combination of Aboriginals who receive services, the federal and relevant provincial governments, and health care providers. Potentially, all Aboriginals could opt into the relevant partnership operating in their province. Specifically, the commission makes the following recommendations:

> Recommendation 42: Current funding for Aboriginal health services provided by the federal, provincial and territorial governments and Aboriginal organizations should be pooled into single consolidated budgets in each province and territory to be used to integrate Aboriginal health care services, improve access, and provide adequate, stable and predictable funding.

> Recommendation 43: The consolidated budgets should be used to fund new Aboriginal Health Partnerships that would be responsible for developing policies, providing services and improving the health of Aboriginal peoples. These partnerships could take

many forms and should reflect the needs, characteristics and circumstances of the population served. (Canada 2002a, 253.)

This option could eliminate differences in the insured services received by Registered Indians and other Aboriginals. It might also simplify somewhat the convoluted channels of financing services that currently exist. On the negative side, however, if such a change extended NIHB to a larger group of Aboriginals beyond Registered Indians, it would offer an obvious fiscal incentive for Aboriginals to opt out of the non-Aboriginal health system, further exacerbating the sense of inequity between Aboriginals and non-Aboriginals over the provision of insured health services. Moreover, it is not clear that the administrative structure proposed would enable those responsible to operate within a "hard" budget constraint and make the tradeoffs necessary to manage a health system.

Give Delivery to the Provinces

To an extent, the idea of transferring responsibility for the delivery of on-reserve health services to the provinces is merely descriptive: as increasing numbers of Indians live off-reserve, the provinces are in any case becoming more involved in providing health services to Aboriginals. The difficulty is, however, that realizing a more formal integration of services would require political sensitivity on the part of the provinces and a breach in the tradition that, on major budgetary matters, bands deal with Ottawa, not the provinces.

Those who argue in favour of this option are persuaded, in part, by the potential for administrative simplification. It would be easier if one order of government organized health services for all residents of a province and thereby eliminated the current convoluted channels for financing. Defence of this option also implies a more subtle thesis: that the government provision of insured health services is an activity that should be undertaken in a manner transparently equal to all, independent of ethnicity.

If the provinces assume responsibility for providing health care services to all of their residents, Aboriginal and non-Aboriginal alike, certain preliminaries need to occur. For example, the provinces might require Ottawa to endorse the principle that treaty obligations do not entail the provision of more generous insured health benefits to Aboriginals than to other Canadians. The provinces would also likely insist that Ottawa transfer fiscal capacity to them in order to reflect the additional costs of providing health services to on-reserve Indians. For its part, Ottawa could insist that bands exercise an advisory role at the provincial level, and it could offer to monitor the changeover to ensure that provinces assume "successorship" responsibilities over arrangements that currently permit bands to influence certain health budgets.[16]

Conclusion

Over the past quarter-century, Aboriginal health outcomes have, in general, improved — the infant-mortality gap between Indians and non-Indians has nearly disappeared. But all is not well. Since 1990, the rate of convergence of life expectancy for the two groups has slowed dramatically. A set of imperfectly understood factors has induced an epidemic of diabetes and sustains an unacceptably high rate of injuries and suicide. There is evidence that the prevalence of AIDS is widening between the two groups.

Perhaps furthering an agenda of institutional parallelism is the appropriate strategy to contend with remaining gaps in health outcomes. My interpretation of the evidence, however, points to two other options. First, integrate delivery of Aboriginal health services with those destined for other Canadians. Second, acknowledge the damaging impact on Aboriginal health outcomes of accommodating low employment rates and recognize that the best health policy is often a jobs policy.

---

16 Another area in need of reform is the gross underrepresentation of Aboriginals among Canada's health care workers, including nurses and physicians. In 1998, it was less than 1 percent of the total, far below the Aboriginal share of Canada's population (Canada 1999). Provincial health departments could more systematically design programs to increase the numbers of Aboriginals in these professions.

Healthy reserve communities need a much better match between the on-reserve adult population and local employment opportunities. The expansion of certain treaty rights — with respect to fishing, for example — can generate some additional on-reserve employment, and in other cases, band councils can negotiate with off-reserve employers to hire band members. But these measures do not suffice. Better matching also requires more off-reserve migration. Bands whose councils concern themselves with employment are more likely to achieve respectable health outcomes. On many reserves, however, employment inevitably will remain dominated by Ottawa-financed services. Using grants from Indian Affairs, councils can organize band offices and other employment-generating facilities, such as schools — useful, well-paid work for a minority. For most others on-reserve, employment options will remain minimal.

Poor employment prospects have many adverse effects. One such is to induce young Aboriginal women to abandon education and the subsequent work world to pursue early parenthood: the on-reserve teenage birth rate is five times that among other Canadians. Another is to trigger psychological syndromes surrounding unemployment. Rendering the world of work more attractive for Aboriginals requires better education outcomes — the subject of the next chapter.

Appendix: Regression Models to Explain Diabetes Prevalence Rates among Aboriginals

In Table A3.1, the dependent variable is the diabetes prevalence rate — taken from the 2001 *Aboriginal Peoples Survey Community Profiles* (Canada 2004a) — among the relevant Aboriginal identity population ages 15 and older. In each region (six provinces plus Atlantic Canada), the on-reserve statistic is a weighted average of the prevalence rates from reporting communities. The weighting factor is the Aboriginal identity population ages 15 and older in each community, relative to the total population of all communities in the region reporting diabetes rates. Since many reserve communities did not supply this information, the on-reserve data are incomplete. Hence, the on-reserve prevalence estimates may be based on non-representative communities and should be treated with caution.

Figure 3.2 illustrates diabetes prevalence rates for the ten cities included in the regression, which are the ten largest urban Aboriginal communities in Canada. All are census metropolitan areas (CMAs) except Prince Albert. The survey also reports off-reserve diabetes prevalence rates for seven provinces: British Columbia, Alberta, Saskatchewan, Manitoba, Ontario, Quebec, and Newfoundland and Labrador. Given the absence of data from the three Maritime provinces, the off-reserve prevalence rate for Atlantic Canada is the statistic for Newfoundland and Labrador, which accounts for two-fifths of Atlantic Canada's Aboriginal population. Given the Aboriginal populations of the ten CMAs and the total off-reserve population outside the CMAs, it is possible to calculate the various off-reserve diabetes prevalence rates used in the regressions.

Employment rates are derived from the *Aboriginal Peoples Survey* (Canada 2003c) and are the proportion of the population over age 15 that was employed during the week prior to Census Day (May 15, 2001). Employment is defined as those who "did any work at all for pay or in self-employment or without pay in a family farm, business or professional practice." It also includes those who would have been employed but, in the week prior to Census Day, were on vacation, ill, or engaged in a labour dispute at their place of work.

Table A3.1: *Regression Models*

	Regression 1	Regression 2	Regression 3	Regression 4	Regression 5
Intercept	6.63****	6.95****	17.17****	4.71****	18.69****
On-reserve (1: population on-reserve; 0: elsewhere)		5.82****		5.76****	
Employment rate *(percent)*			–0.17***		–0.25****
Alberta (1: population in Alberta; 0: elsewhere)	0.004			0.48	1.54
Saskatchewan (1: population in Saskatchewan; 0: elsewhere)	1.59			2.36*	0.11
Manitoba (1: population in Manitoba; 0: elsewhere)	3.60			3.60**	3.36**
Ontario (1: population in Ontario; 0: elsewhere)	3.99*			4.47***	6.49*
Quebec (1: population in Quebec; 0: elsewhere)	1.42			1.42	1.46
Atlantic Canada (1: population in Atlantic Canada; 0: elsewhere)	4.70*			3.74**	2.88
R-square	0.21	0.51	0.25	0.69	0.56
R-square, adjusted	–0.07	0.49	0.21	0.56	0.37

Note: Level of significance is indicated by the following legend:
*   0.25 significance (two-tail t-test)
**   0.15 significance (two-tail t-test)
***   0.05 significance (two-tail t-test)
****   0.01 significance (two-tail t-test)

4 *Schools Matter*

The Industrial Revolution has permitted dramatic increases in per capita incomes, from nineteenth-century Manchester to twenty-first-century Shanghai. Often, however, it has also painfully disrupted old ways of living and doing things. One of the most painful of those disruptions is that endured by the trapping-hunting-fishing societies of North American Aboriginals.

The essence of the Industrial Revolution is the systematic application of new technologies to work. As industrial technologies have become more complex, the role of formal education has become more important. The benefits of formal education extend, of course, well beyond the narrowly economic. Universal education has been crucial to the emancipation of women, enabling them to pursue careers other than — or in addition to — parenting. And successful democracies need a free press and citizens able to read it, and thereby to understand the broad political issues at stake.

Elites have understood the value of formal education for millennia and their incomes have usually enabled them to acquire it for their children. In the absence of publicly provided education, only a minority among non-elites are able to, or choose to, make the necessary sacrifices for their children's education. No nation, in fact, has succeeded in preparing its citizens sufficiently for a modern industrial economy without providing universal public education — and the provision of such education is now considered a core responsibility of government.

The importance of a country's having an educated, literate population is acknowledged by the United Nations in its Human Development Index. Each country's index value is based on its per capita income, its life expectancy, and two measures of its education performance: literacy and school enrollment rates. In constructing the index this way, the UN is doing more than simply acknowledging the centrality of a good primary education system to any developing economy. The literacy component also indicates the fraction of a country's population that, lacking education, is likely to be left behind, condemned to low-paying occupations, even if the national economy prospers.

In wealthy industrial societies like Canada, enjoying the benefits of development requires more than simple literacy. Today, one needs, at the minimum, to have completed secondary education, while earning a "good" income increasingly requires some post-secondary training. Most Aboriginals have education levels that are too low to permit them to earn a "good" income. The result is high Aboriginal poverty rates.

Many historical factors enter into explanations of low Aboriginal education levels. History has, for example, made it harder for Aboriginal communities than for many other groups to champion the importance of educational achievement; in this regard, the legacy of family disruptions occasioned by residential schools looms large. But if Aboriginals are to escape poverty, they must become better educated. As I hope to demonstrate in this chapter, the links among education, employment, and income hold as much for Aboriginals as they do for other Canadians. I also take advantage of the data available on Aboriginal student performance in British Columbia to focus on the situation among Aboriginal students attending that province's schools. I finish the chapter with an assessment of options for improving Aboriginal education outcomes.[1]

---

1 This chapter draws heavily on Richards and Vining (2004).

Education, Work, and Income

To begin to understand the links among education, employment, and income, it is worth looking at a snapshot of income distribution among Aboriginals and comparing it with the distribution among non-Aboriginals. Using data from the *Aboriginal Peoples Survey* (Canada 2003c), Figure 4.1 illustrates income distributions in 2000 among the 25-to-44 and 45-to-64 age cohorts, but in the case of off-reserve Aboriginals makes a distinction between those who are Aboriginal by identity and those who are Aboriginal by ethnic origin.[2] The reader must bear in mind that these distributions refer to individuals, not to families. They do not take into account the number of dependents an individual supports, nor do they include income-in-kind — such as access to band-supplied housing — a category of income much more important for those on-reserve than off-reserve.

For both age cohorts, Aboriginal median incomes are well below those of non-Aboriginals. This is emphatically so among the on-reserve population, whose median income is less than half that of non-Aboriginals. If one informally defines those with annual income below $20,000 as poor, nearly two-thirds of the on-reserve population, but only one-third of the non-Aboriginal population, are poor. By this admittedly imprecise measure, the poverty rate among off-reserve Aboriginals lies roughly halfway between those for on-reserve Aboriginals and non-Aboriginals. Indeed, the poverty rate among off-reserve Aboriginals by ethnic origin is closer to that for non-Aboriginals than to the rate for the on-reserve population.

---

2   The "identity" definition of Aboriginals refers to those persons who reported in the census as identifying with at least one Aboriginal group (North American Indian, Métis, or Inuit), even though they may not necessarily have Aboriginal ancestry. Thus, to some extent, "identity" is a matter of individual choice. The economic fortunes of an individual with one or two Aboriginal parents but who chooses not to identify as Aboriginal are as important as those of someone who embraces his or her cultural heritage. Among those living on-reserve, the difference between the Aboriginal identity count and the Aboriginal origin count is negligible. Among those living off-reserve, however, roughly three report themselves as Aboriginal in terms of origin for every two who report an Aboriginal identity — hence the usefulness of showing these two groups separately in Figure 4.1.

Figure 4.1: *Income Distributions, Aboriginals On- and Off-Reserve and Non-Aboriginals, 2000*

A.   *Ages 25 to 44*

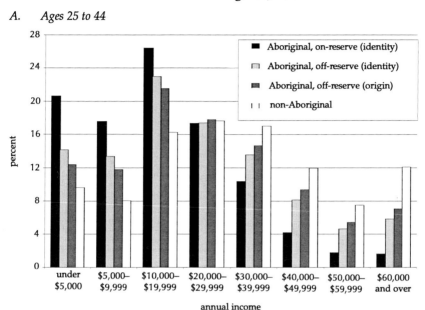

B.   *Ages 45 to 64*

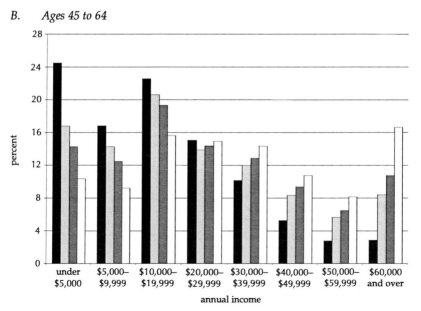

Source: Canada 2003c.

If one defines prosperity to mean an annual income above $50,000 — a low threshold — a quarter of the older cohort and a fifth of the younger cohort of non-Aboriginals qualify. The corresponding proportions among the on-reserve populations are very low: 6 percent for the older cohort and 3 percent for the younger. Similar to the poverty rate, the prosperity rate among off-reserve Aboriginals lies between those for on-reserve populations and non-Aboriginals.

Another way of interpreting the distributions in Figure 4.1 is to use the median income of non-Aboriginals to define economic success. As Table 4.1 shows, according to the 2001 Census, just over a third of individuals who identify themselves as Aboriginals and live off-reserve had incomes above the non-Aboriginal median, as did a slightly higher fraction of Aboriginal-origin individuals living off-reserve. By contrast, only a fifth of Aboriginals living on-reserve enjoyed incomes above the non-Aboriginal median.

What emerges from these income distributions is that off-reserve Aboriginal populations are considerably more prosperous than those on-reserve. Why such large differences among Aboriginals? The most important explanation, as the following section explores in some detail, is in their relative levels of employment and education.

The Link between Work and Income

Figure 4.2 draws from the 2001 Census to illustrate the relationship between employment and income among selected groups of Canadians in their prime earning years between the ages of 25 and 44.[3] Those in this age group are old enough to have completed their education and training, and young enough to have benefited from the emphasis on formal education over the past four decades: the oldest entered school in the early 1960s, the youngest in the early 1980s. The figure plots the relationship between income and the employment rate for this age cohort, but separated into six provincial

---

3   These data are derived from the 2001 *Aboriginal Peoples Survey* (Canada 2003c), part of the 2001 Census. For discussion of the meaning and limitations of the census income concept in the context of Aboriginal surveys, see Drost and Richards (2003).

Table 4.1: *Measuring Economic Success, Aboriginals*
On- and Off-Reserve and Non-Aboriginals, 2000

	Aboriginals			Non-Aboriginals
	On-Reserve Identity	Off-Reserve Identity	Off-Reserve Origin	
Ages 24 to 44				
Median income, 2000 ($)	13,800	19,700	22,000	29,000
Share with incomes				
below $20,000 (%)	65	51	46	34
above $50,000 (%)	3	10	12	20
above non-Aboriginal median (%)	20	34	38	50
Ages 45 to 64				
Median income, 2000 ($)	12,800	18,800	22,300	29,900
Share with incomes				
below $20,000 (%)	64	52	46	35
above $50,000 (%)	6	14	17	25
above non-Aboriginal median (%)	21	35	40	50

Source: Author's calculations from 2003c.

groupings (the six provinces with substantial Aboriginal populations); either Aboriginal or non-Aboriginal; and, for the Aboriginal populations, by residence either on- or off-reserve. This division thus allocates each of six provinces' population ages 25 to 44 into one of three categories — 18 groups in all.

As the figure reveals, the link between employment and income exists among the various Aboriginal groups as much as it does between Aboriginals and non-Aboriginals. Unambiguously the poorest of the 18 groups are on-reserve Aboriginals living in the Prairie provinces, where median incomes in 2000 were less than $12,000 and employment rates were below 45 percent. The average of the median incomes of the six off-reserve groups was about 45 percent higher than that of the six on-reserve groups. The wealthiest Aboriginals, those living off-reserve in Ontario, enjoyed twice the median income of on-reserve Prairie Aboriginals. In turn, the six non-Aboriginal groups had, on average, median incomes that were about

Figure 4.2: *Median Incomes of Aboriginals On- and Off-Reserve and Non-Aboriginals, Ages 25–44, Selected Provinces, by Employment Rate, 2000*

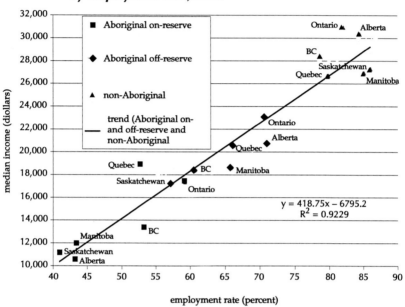

Source: Canada 2003c.

45 percent higher than those of off-reserve Aboriginals. A trend line across all 18 groups reveals that a ten-percentage-point increase in the employment rate is accompanied by an increase of nearly $4,200 in the median income.

   In allowing individuals to escape poverty, employment clearly matters a great deal. But to get a good job, education matters more now than in generations past. A century ago, the large fraction of the labour force employed in Canada's forests, factories, and mines earned good wages regardless of formal education. In the twenty-first century, far fewer such jobs exist. Aggravating the implication of this trend, low-end wages have risen more slowly over the past half-century than high-end wages, resulting in greater wage dispersion (see OECD 1996). For anyone now entering the labour force, limited formal education means fewer job opportunities and wages even lower than average in the jobs available than in decades past.

That the link between education level and income applies as much to Aboriginals as to others in the labour force is evident from Figure 4.3, which again divides the Aboriginal population into those living on- and off-reserve:[4] as the education level of Aboriginals rises, so does their median income. The figure also reveals that there are, among off-reserve Aboriginals and non-Aboriginals but less evident among on-reserve Aboriginals, three educational steps. The first step up, in terms of increased income, takes place upon completion of high school, which is now the minimum qualification for many entry-level jobs.[5] Those who aspire to reasonably well paying jobs need to reach at least the second step, completion of a trade certificate. The third step is completion of a university degree.

Again looking at the 18 groups of 25-to-44-year-olds from the 2001 Census, the employment rate obviously rises with education level, as Figure 4.4 illustrates in terms of high school graduation.[6] A higher education level leads to the possibility of a better-paying job, the rewards from which are likely to outweigh those from non-work options, such as social assistance.

Two Snapshots of Off-Reserve Aboriginals

Two recent Statistics Canada studies of social conditions among off-reserve Aboriginals offer further evidence of the links among education, employment, and income. From one study looking at Aboriginal employment in the four western provinces (Canada 2005a)

---

4 For studies that consider education achievement and income distributions among ethnic groups, see Antecol and Bedard (2002); Bradbury (2002); Drolet (2002); and Pendakur and Pendakur (2002).

5 Using 1996 Census data for Saskatchewan, Howe (2002) estimates that expected lifetime financial returns to Aboriginals who complete high school are much larger than expected incomes of Aboriginals who fail to do so.

6 This correlation between education and employment exists whether the measure of education is the percentage with high school graduation or higher, or the percentage with a trade certificate or higher. For Aboriginals on-reserve, those with trade certificates tend to have higher employment rates than those with high school graduation. Many of the relatively few, usually band-council-financed, on-reserve jobs require some postsecondary education.

Figure 4.3: *Median Incomes of Aboriginals On- and Off-Reserve and Non-Aboriginals, by Level of Education, 1995*

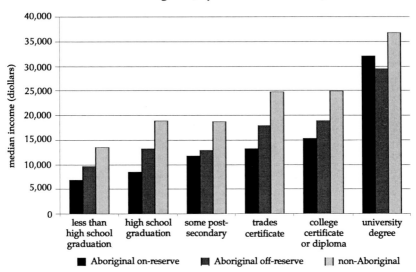

Source: Author's calcuations, as reported in Drost and Richards 2003.

comes the good news that employment rates among off-reserve Aboriginals with completed postsecondary education and those among non-Aboriginals with comparable education differ by a single percentage point: 82.5 versus 83.5 percent. There is more good news. At just 1.5 percentage points, the employment gap between non-Aboriginals and Métis has almost closed. Albertans have a reputation as hard workers; their employment rate is traditionally the highest of the ten provinces. In another sign of success, the employment rate among off-reserve Alberta Aboriginals — including here both those identifying as Indian and as Métis — now exceeds the rate among non-Aboriginals in British Columbia (see Figure 4.5).

Although off-reserve Aboriginal employment rates have improved since the 2001 Census, this study also reveals serious remaining gaps:

- Young off-reserve Aboriginals ages 15 to 24 have an employment rate far below that of young non-Aboriginals: 44 versus 62 percent.

Figure 4.4: *Employment Rate, Aboriginals On- and Off-Reserve and Non-Aboriginals, Ages 25–44, Selected Provinces, by Percentage with High School Graduation Certificate or Higher Education, 2001*

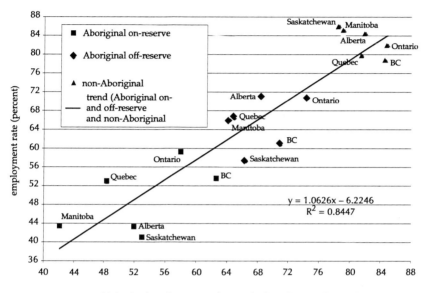

Source: Canada 2003c.

- Overall, the employment rate remains much higher for non-Aboriginals than for off-reserve Indians: 65 versus 50 percent. Racism may play a role in explaining low Indian employment rates, but the major factor undoubtedly is low education levels — which reflect the inadequacies of provincially run and band-run schools for Indian children.
- · Employment rates are particularly low among off-reserve Aboriginals in Saskatchewan: 8 percentage points lower than in the neighbouring province of Manitoba.

The second Statistics Canada report (Siggner and Costa 2005) examines changes in social outcomes among off-reserve Aboriginals

Figure 4.5: *Off-Reserve Employment Rate by Racial Identity,*
Western Provinces, April 2004–March 2005

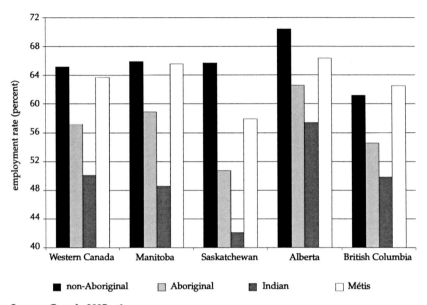

Source: Canada 2005a, 6.

in 11 Canadian cities between 1981 and 2001.[7] One such outcome is
the level of education among young Aboriginal adults. Measured
by the proportion with a high school certificate or higher, Aboriginal youth are catching up, although a gap remains. As Figure 4.6
shows, increases in Aboriginal education levels generally exceeded
those of non-Aboriginals over the two decades — in nine of 11 cities
in the case of women, in six of 11 in the case of men. Clearly,
improvements have been more significant for girls than for boys.

---

7   Over the two decades, the Aboriginal identity population more than doubled
    in these 11 cities. Siggner and Costa (2005) decompose this increase into natural
    increase (births less deaths), net migration, changes in underreporting, and "ethnic
    migration." As social stigma against Aboriginals diminishes and Canadians
    accord Aboriginal culture more respect, increasing numbers of people choose
    to identify themselves as Aboriginal in Census counts. This "migration" in
    ethnic identity explains roughly half the population increase since 1981. It
    likely also explains some of the improvement in education levels, as larger
    numbers of relatively educated young people identify as Aboriginal.

Figure 4.6: *Increases in Education Attainment, Aboriginals and Non-Aboriginals, by Sex, Selected Cities, 1981–2001*

A. *Males ages 20–24, not in school*

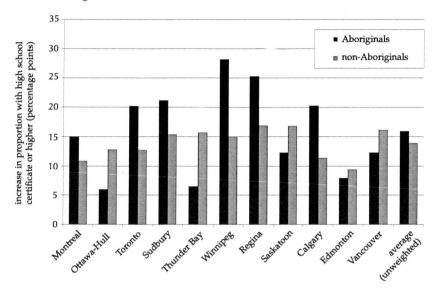

B. *Females ages 20–24, not in school*

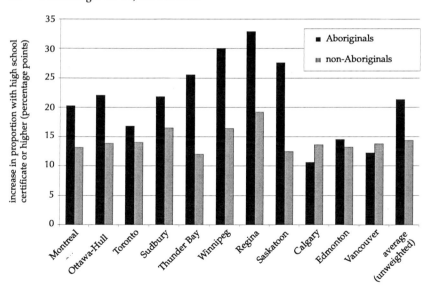

Source: Siggner and Costa 2005.

Table 4.2: *Aboriginal and Non-Aboriginal Population Ages 20–24 not Attending School and with High School Graduation or Higher Education, by Sex, Selected Cities, 1981 and 2001*

	Aboriginal				Non-Aboriginal			
	Males		Females		Males		Females	
	1981	2001	1981	2001	1981	2001	1981	2001
			(percent)					
Montreal	64.3	79.3	67.2	87.4	75.1	85.9	78.0	91.1
Ottawa–Hull	70.0	76.0	65.4	87.4	76.2	89.0	79.9	93.8
Toronto	54.2	74.4	64.2	81.0	75.2	87.9	78.6	92.6
Sudbury	52.9	74.1	59.3	81.1	74.1	89.4	75.4	91.9
Thunder Bay	69.7	76.2	44.4	69.9	71.0	86.7	78.1	90.1
Winnipeg	34.5	62.7	37.6	67.6	69.0	84.0	73.3	89.7
Regina	47.5	72.8	32.8	65.7	68.6	85.5	72.9	92.1
Saskatoon	44.8	57.1	42.4	70.0	67.8	84.6	77.2	89.7
Calgary	47.3	67.6	58.8	69.4	72.6	83.9	76.0	89.6
Edmonton	50.0	57.9	52.2	66.7	71.9	81.3	75.3	88.5
Vancouver	54.6	66.9	65.6	77.8	73.1	89.2	79.0	92.8
Averages (unweighted)	53.6	69.5	53.6	74.9	72.2	86.1	76.7	91.1

Source: Siggner and Costa 2005.

As Table 4.2 indicates, in 1981 the proportion of young Aboriginal women and men in these cities with high school graduation certification was the same. By 2001, a five-percentage-point gap had emerged in favour of women. (A gender gap of similar size also exists among non-Aboriginals.) Accompanying the increases in Aboriginal education levels, Siggner and Costa also find that median earnings among Aboriginals increased relative to those among non-Aboriginals in eight of the 11 cities in their study (see Figure 4.7).

A Summary of the Education-Income Link

Figure 4.8 provides a summary of the evidence on the link between education and income. The explanation for a positive link is twofold: higher education increases the employment rate, and it increases earnings among those who are employed. The slope of the trend line among the 12 Aboriginal groups implies that a ten-percentage-

Figure 4.7: *Ratios of Aboriginal to Non-Aboriginal Median Employment Incomes, Selected Cities, 1980 and 2000*

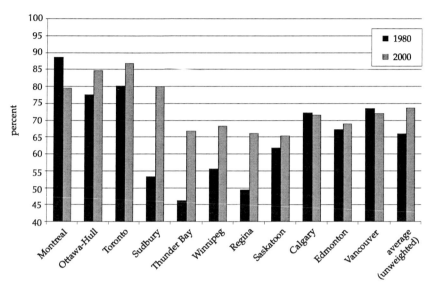

Source: Siggner and Costa 2005.

point increase in the Aboriginal high school completion rate increases annual median income by $2,900. Admittedly, a satisfactory explanation of comparative incomes requires a far more complex story than reference to high school completion. As Figure 4.8 shows, particularly among the on-reserve populations, there are outliers: Alberta, Saskatchewan, and British Columbia are well below the trend line; Quebec is well above.

Education and Location of Residence

Registered Indians, who make up the majority of Aboriginals who identify in the Census as Indians — as opposed to Métis or Inuit — can choose to live either on- or off-reserve. On-reserve, they can participate more readily in the cultural life of the tribe, but the scarcity of well-paying jobs on or near most reserves means that Indians who live there have fewer incentives to invest in formal education than their off-reserve relatives. This self-selection dynamic

Figure 4.8: *Median Incomes, Aboriginals On- and Off-Reserve and Non-Aboriginals, Ages 25-44, Selected Provinces, by Percentage with High School Graduation Certificate or Higher Education, 2000*

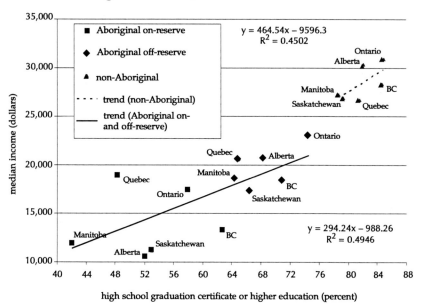

Source: Canada 2003c.

is probably important in explaining low on-reserve education levels; it is also probably part of the explanation for the underperformance of on-reserve schools.

Even if many on-reserve adults willingly forgo off-reserve employment opportunities, on-reserve education attainment remains an important issue if their children are to be able to make a realistic choice, when the time comes, between an on- or off-reserve lifestyle. Figures 4.9–4.11 draw from the 2001 Census, which allows for a finer examination of education achievements by area of residence, ethnic identity, and age cohorts than was formerly available. The youngest cohort for which census education data are available is those ages 15 to 24, which permits a tentative forecast of education levels among the next generation, although the evidence is obviously incomplete — many in this cohort are still in school or undertaking

Figure 4.9: *High School Certificate or Higher Education,*
by Identity Group and Area of Residence, 2001

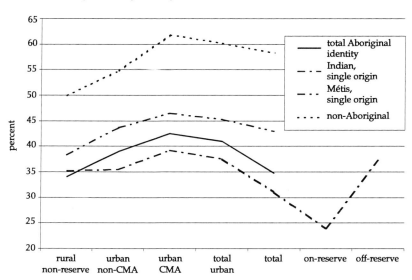

Source: Canada 2003c.

some form of postsecondary instruction. Figure 4.9 shows, by place of residence, the percentage of 15-to-24-year-olds among the Aboriginal population with a high school education or better. For comparison, the non-Aboriginal cohort is included. For all identity categories, education levels are highest in large cities (census metropolitan areas, labeled "urban CMA" in Figure 4.9). The results for small cities are somewhat lower, rural non-reserve results are lower yet, and the lowest results are for Indians on-reserve.

So far, we have looked mostly at high school attainment levels among Aboriginals, but a more comprehensive survey of their education profiles, both on- and off-reserve, is revealing. Figure 4.10 summarizes education attainment levels of all Aboriginals and non-Aboriginals ages 15 years and older, as well as for those ages 15 to 24, 25 to 44, and 45 to 64. Figure 4.11 shows the differences between the education levels of the 25-to-44 and 45-to-64 age cohorts of on- and off-reserve Aboriginals and non-Aboriginals.

Figure 4.10: *Education Profiles of Aboriginals On- and
Off-Reserve and Non-Aboriginals, 2001*

A.   *Ages 15 and older*

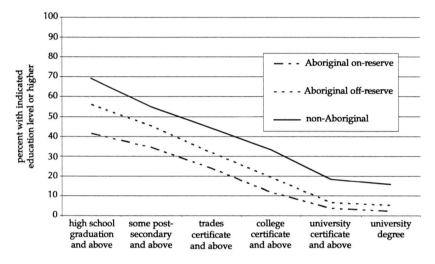

Source: Author's calculations from Canada 2003c.

B.   *Ages 15 to 24*

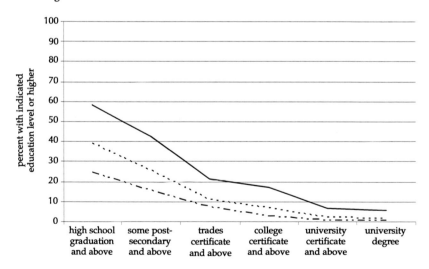

Source: Author's calculations from Canada 2003c.

Figure 4.10 - continued

C.   *Ages 25 to 44*

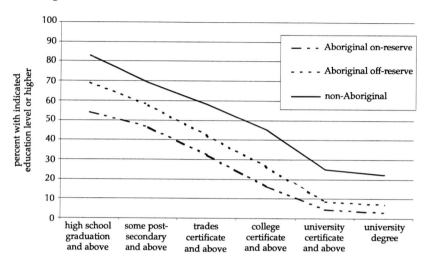

Source: Author's calculations from Canada 2003c.

D.   *Ages 45 to 64*

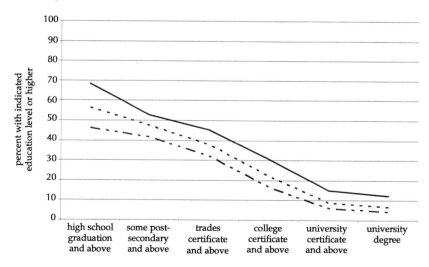

Source: Author's calculations from Canada 2003c.

Figure 4.11: *Changes in Education Profiles of Aboriginals*
On- and Off-Reserve and Non-Aboriginals,
25-to-44 Age Cohort less 45-to-64 Age Cohort, 2001

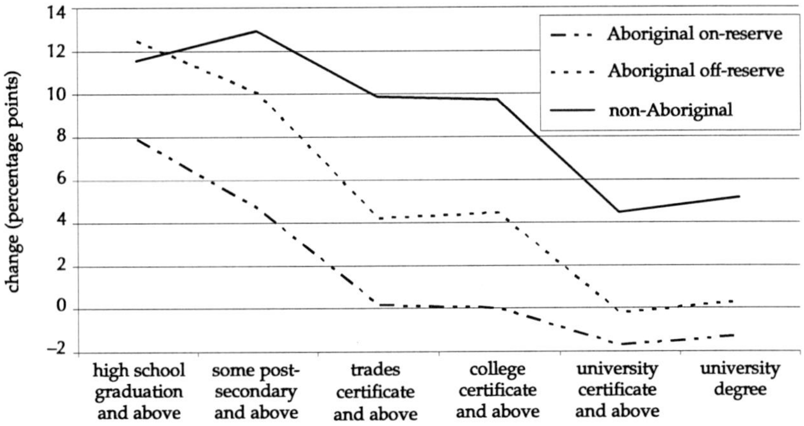

Source: Author's calculations from Canada 2003c.

The good news is that, as far as high school graduation rates are concerned, 25-to-44-year-old Aboriginals are better educated than those ages 45 to 64.[8] The bad news is that younger cohorts have not made comparable improvements at the higher education levels. Among off-reserve Aboriginals, the proportion with trades certificates (or better) is somewhat higher for 25-to-44-year-olds than for the older cohort. Among on-reserve Aboriginals, there is no intergenerational improvement at this education level. Among both on- and off-reserve Aboriginals, the proportions with university degrees are essentially unchanged across age cohorts. Except at the high school graduation level, improvements among younger non-Aboriginals clearly dominate any analogous improvements for Aboriginals. In conclusion, there appears to be no intergenerational convergence of Aboriginal to non-Aboriginal education profiles at levels above high school graduation.

Indeed, as Figure 4.10, panel B, shows disconcertingly, 15-to-24-year-old Aboriginals are proportionately further behind the education

---

8   As with the 1981 to 2001 comparisons discussed earlier, some portion of the improvement by the younger cohort may be due to changing patterns of identity.

Schools Matter

75

attainments of the generation ahead of them than are 15-to-24-year-old non-Aboriginals.⁹ At a minimum, here is evidence that should prompt a sense of urgency among those responsible for Aboriginal education. Low Aboriginal education outcomes are condemning the next generation to poverty.

What to Do about Aboriginal Education

Switching from description to policy, the obvious question to pose is, how can education levels be improved? Band control of on-reserve schools may have contributed to improved results since the 1969 White Paper; it is not a panacea. Education outcomes are lower among on-reserve Aboriginals than among those off-reserve and, as we have seen, young 15-to-24-year-old on-reserve Aboriginals are not making acceptable educational progress.

In 2000, Canada's Auditor General documented the glacial pace at which high school completion rates for on-reserve Aboriginals and non-Aboriginals were converging (Canada 2000b). The report admonished the federal Department of Indian Affairs on "the need to articulate its role in education, to develop and use appropriate performance measures and to improve operational performance" (4–5). In the 2004 report, the Auditor General returned to the issue, in a tone of frustration at the department's lack of urgency and

---

9   For example, non-Aboriginal 15-to-24 year-olds have achieved 70 percent of the high school and above level of the non-Aboriginal cohort ages 25 to 44 (70 percent = 58.3 percent / 82.9 percent). On-reserve 15-to-24-year-old Aboriginals have realized only 45 percent of the comparable level among on-reserve 25-to-44-year-olds (45 percent = 24.2 percent / 54.2 percent). Off-reserve, the ratio is 57 percent. Similar results exist at higher education levels. Does this evidence mean young Aboriginals are slipping back relative to the education attainment of the generation ahead of them? Not necessarily, since the evidence from the 15-to-24-year-old cohort is incomplete. Obviously, we do not know the future, but it could turn out that Aboriginals complete their education on average at an older age than do non-Aboriginals, in which case the data for 15-to-24-year-olds represent proportionately less of the ultimate education attainment of Aboriginals than of non-Aboriginals.

dissatisfaction with its "hands-off" interpretation of its role (Canada 2004c, s.5.22). Noting that, according to 2001 Census data, convergence rates had slowed, the report castigated the department's reluctance to evaluate on-reserve school outcomes:

> At the operational level, we found there is still ambiguity and inconsistency in the role of regional offices in fulfilling the Department's mandate and achieving its education objectives. The Department expects that the education delivered in schools located on reserves is comparable with what provinces offer off reserves and that students are able to transfer from band-operated to provincial schools without academic penalty. However, a number of school evaluations we reviewed clearly indicated that some students do not perform at their current grade level, suggesting that they cannot transfer to the same grade in the provincial education system. Yet, we saw no evidence that the regions consider this information in assessing whether First Nations meet the terms and conditions of their funding agreement and whether corrective action is required. Most regions continue to interpret their major role as that of providing a funding service. (s.5.37.)

With qualifications, the Auditor General's concerns also apply to the provinces. Aboriginal students attending provincially run schools outnumber those going to band-run reserve schools by nearly four to one. Furthermore, the school systems are not watertight compartments: Aboriginal families are much more mobile than most Canadians, and above-average numbers of Aboriginal students change schools, both within provincial systems and between on- and off-reserve schools. In both systems, high Aboriginal family mobility has a damaging effect on student performance.[10] Despite honourable exceptions, too many local school boards and provincial education ministries remain fatalistic about Aboriginal education outcomes. They are not exerting themselves to find out what is happening to Aboriginal students within their jurisdiction. They are reluctant to publish detailed school-by-school results.

---

10 See Richards (2001) for a review of evidence on Aboriginal student mobility.

Canada's Senate has also weighed in with an analysis of weak Aboriginal educational achievement in a report on urban youth (Canada 2003d):

> There are many complex reasons why youth stop attending school. Some of these reasons include: racism; lack of parental involvement and guidance; resentment and embarrassment caused by feeling less successful scholastically than other students; instability caused by high rates of residential mobility; feelings of isolation caused by being in environments that are not culturally sensitive; an inability to afford text books, sporting equipment, and excursion fees; an unstable home life; and poverty.
>
> Consistently, witnesses emphasized that the lack of parental involvement, guidance and support was partly responsible for the fact that Aboriginal youth continue to fare so poorly academically....
>
> The damaging effects of residential schools on Aboriginal peoples, cultures, and languages are now widely recognized.... [T]here is a deep mistrust among some Aboriginal people of mainstream educational institutions. The importance of obtaining a good education becomes secondary to what may be perceived as a further assimilative assault on Aboriginal culture, language and traditions. (s.1.4.)

The primary focus of the Senate report was the problems of poor, inner-city neighbourhoods, where Aboriginals are disproportionately likely to live (Richards 2001). Fortunately, many urban Aboriginals are succeeding, but the senators are right: closing the education gap, particularly in poor neighbourhoods, will not be easy. But if more Aboriginals are to escape poverty, it is a gap that must be closed.

There is no inherent contradiction in studying the importance of Louis Riel in Prairie history *and* mastering geometry. What community leaders, both Aboriginal and non-Aboriginal, need to do is encourage learning that embodies both Aboriginal culture *and* the core academic skills and knowledge that contemporary society requires. Translating this obligation into pragmatic policy, however, means measuring school performance — championing the good and reforming the weak.

Aboriginal Students in
British Columbia Schools

There is one exception to the critique made earlier that provinces are reluctant to publish data on performance of Aboriginal students in provincial schools. Since the late 1990s, the British Columbia education ministry has published a wealth of relevant information. In the 2002–03 school year, 49,000 students in the BC school system — 8.2 percent of the total student count — identified themselves as Aboriginals. Of the Aboriginal students who entered grade 8 in 1996, 42.5 percent graduated from high school within six years, compared with 79.2 percent of non-Aboriginals (see Figure 4.12).[11] Although Aboriginal high school completion rates are low, there has been improvement in recent years. For example, the 1996 Aboriginal cohort had a completion rate that was 8.7 percentage points higher than that of the Aboriginal cohort that entered grade 8 in 1991. Moreover, between 1991 and 1996, Aboriginal students closed slightly the gap between their high school completion rate and the non-Aboriginal rate, which increased by 6.4 percentage points (British Columbia 2003, 26).

Quality of schooling matters as much as quantity. The importance of measuring school quality and of providing incentives to schools to perform better is a recurring theme in contemporary education policy analysis.[12] Over the past decade and following an international trend, many provinces have set up province-wide tests intended to measure performance in core subjects at various stages

---

11 Of course, some would have left the province and others will finish high school at a later date. However, as Cowley and Easton (2004, 13) point out, although such adjustments apply disproportionately to Aboriginal students, they are minor and do not affect the overall conclusion that dropout rates for Aboriginal students are unacceptably high.

12 Hanushek (2002) offers an excellent survey of empirical studies of the outcomes of policies to improve school performance. Bishop (1997, 2001) has written extensively on the value of jurisdiction-wide tests on core subjects as means to improve average school system performance by providing information to parents, students, and teachers on a basis that permits comparison across schools and among all children.

Figure 4.12: *Student Retention and Graduation Rates,*
BC Provincial Schools, Cohort Entering Grade 8 in 1996

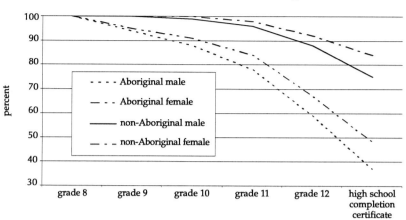

Source: British Columbia 2003.

of students' careers. Since 1999, British Columbia's education ministry has organized annual province-wide Foundation Skills Assessment (FSA) tests in reading, writing, and numeracy for nearly all students in grades 4, 7, and 10.[13]

Students who take the FSA tests receive one of three results: "not meeting expectations," "meeting expectations," or "exceeding expectations." To preserve confidentiality, results are not reported for individual students, but they are available at the level of the individual school. In addition, each school's results are reported by a number of student characteristics, including whether the student identifies as being Aboriginal.[14] The most frequently used statistic from these tests is the "meet/exceed" score, which is the percentage of student tests in a school or larger unit that "meet" or "exceed" expectations. The score may refer to a particular grade, to a particular subject, to boys or girls, and so on.

---

13 Subsequent to the years under review, British Columbia has organized province-wide exams in core subjects in grade 10 in lieu of FSA tests.

14 Readers interested in the Aboriginal education performance of individual BC schools should look at Cowley and Easton (2004), who provide a great deal of useful information beyond the FSA results.

If the quality of schools matters, as it undoubtedly does in explaining student performance, it is important to look at how particular schools are faring in terms of their Aboriginal students. Since the FSA program began in the 1999–2000 school year, approximately 400 BC schools have annually reported results that include Aboriginal as well as non-Aboriginal students. A useful measure among these "mixed schools" is the meet/exceed score, for Aboriginal and non-Aboriginal students, respectively, in a particular school. This statistic averages FSA results within a particular school over all relevant grades and all test components.

Figure 4.13 shows the distributions of both Aboriginal and non-Aboriginal school meet/exceed scores in 391 mixed schools for the four school years 1999–2000 to 2002–03.[15] Consider the distributions of scores ranked from high to low. At the upper end, the gap between Aboriginal and non-Aboriginal results is fairly small. At the ninth decile — by definition, the point at which 10 percent of schools perform better and 90 percent perform worse — the gap is somewhat over 8 percentage points. Moving down to schools performing less well, deciles diverge dramatically: the median school score for non-Aboriginal students is 16 percentage points higher than the median score for Aboriginal students, while in the first decile — the point at which 90 percent of schools perform better and 10 percent perform worse — the gap reaches 25 percentage points.

Some schools — including some in which Aboriginal scores are more than a fifth of the total — are doing well by their Aboriginal students. If one defines "doing well" to mean a school's Aboriginal meet/exceed score is above the non-Aboriginal median, 30 of the 391 schools qualify; unfortunately, the great majority do not.

Figure 4.14 shows the result of a similar exercise among the 391 schools in which school scores are calculated in terms of the percentage of FSA scores that exceed expectations. Once again, the score averages FSA results within a school over all relevant grades and

---

15 For the 391 mixed schools included in these distributions, school rankings differ for the Aboriginal and non-Aboriginal scores.

Figure 4.13: *"Meet/Exceed" Decile and Minimum-Maximum Scores for Aboriginal and Non-Aboriginal Students in Mixed BC Schools, academic years 1999–2000 to 2002–03*

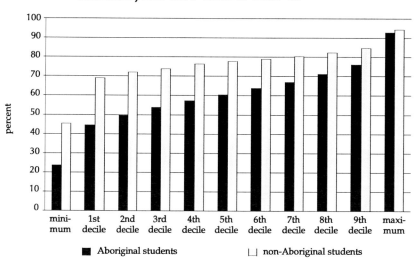

Note: The distributions include 391 schools. Each of these schools reported both Aboriginal and non-Aboriginal FSA scores for at least three of the four school years. The BC Department of Education has recently revised procedures for designation of Aboriginal students. These revisions are not reflected in these calculations. See the text for definitions of mixed schools, school meet/exceed scores, and school exceed scores. The correlation between the school meet/exceed scores for Aboriginal and non-Aboriginal students is 0.51. The analogous correlation between school exceed scores is 0.34.

Source: Author's calculations from FSA data provided by the BC Department of Education.

test components. In 40 schools, the maximum score was actually slightly higher for Aboriginal students than for non-Aboriginal students. In general, however, results are not satisfactory. At all deciles, the school exceed scores for Aboriginal students are well below the analogous decile scores for non-Aboriginals. In nearly a quarter of the 391 schools there were no Aboriginal "exceeds expectations" scores, whereas only two schools recorded no "exceeds expectations" among their non-Aboriginal students.

Why do Aboriginal students fare so much worse in some schools than in others — or, to be optimistic, why do Aboriginal students fare so much better in some schools than in others? The statistics

Figure 4.14: *"Exceed" Decile and Minimum-Maximum Scores for Aboriginal and Non-Aboriginal Students in Mixed BC Schools, academic years 1999–2000 to 2002–03*

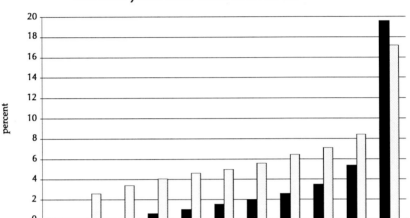

Source: Author's calculations from FSA data provided by the BC Department of Education.

assembled in Table 4.3 afford a number of insights. The school groupings — from bottom tenth to top tenth — are constructed by ranking a sample of mixed schools by their Aboriginal FSA school meet/exceed scores for the 2000–01 school year. The first column presents average Aboriginal FSA meet/exceed scores for schools within each group, while the second column does the same for non-Aboriginal scores. The third column gives the average Aboriginal share of total scores among schools within each group. The remaining five columns display relevant statistics for neighbourhood characteristics. As the table shows, average Aboriginal meet/exceed scores ranged from 31 percent in the bottom tenth of schools to 91 percent in the top tenth. Although the data do not allow for assessment of individual family characteristics on individual student outcomes, it is possible to consider the effect of the socio-economic characteristics of the school's catchment area — the census tract (or tracts) in which the school and its immediate neighbourhood are located and from which the school draws its students.

Table 4.3: *Racial and Neighbourhood Characteristics,*
Sample of Mixed BC Schools, academic year 2000–01
(averages by school cohort, ranked by Aboriginal FSA meet/exceed scores)

	School Racial Characteristics		
School Cohorts[a]	Aboriginal Meet/Exceed Score (1)	Non-Aboriginal Meet/Exceed Score (2)	Aboriginal Share of Total Student Scores (3)
	(percent)		
Bottom tenth	30.5	63.1	17.8
Bottom quarter	39.4	68.3	19.5
Second quarter	56.4	74.4	11.2
Third quarter	68.0	76.5	10.4
Top quarter	82.9	82.8	9.3
Top tenth	90.7	83.8	9.8

	School Neighbourhood Characteristics				
School Cohorts[a]	Average Family Income[b] (4)	Poverty Rate[c] (5)	Lone-Parent Families[d] (6)	Family Head with Trade Certificate or Higher (7)	School in "Very Poor Neighbourhood"[e] (8)
	(dollars)	(percent)	(percent)	(percent)	(percent)
Bottom tenth	45,097	22.0	19.1	47.6	13.3
Bottom quarter	45,262	22.5	20.0	47.8	15.8
Second quarter	49,517	17.9	16.7	51.2	8.1
Third quarter	48,163	17.6	15.5	49.4	10.8
Top quarter	50,124	14.4	14.7	50.6	0.0
Top tenth	49,519	16.0	14.0	50.6	0.0

[a] Schools are ranked by average meet/exceed score of all aboriginal students in the school; averages are calculated for schools in the relevant school cohort.

[b] Average family income in a school neighbourhood refers to the relevant weighted mean total income of census families. The income of a census family includes the total 1995 incomes of all family members ages 15 and older.

[c] The neighbourhood poverty rate is the percentage of families below the relevant Statistics Canada low-income cut-off (LICO).

[d] Total number of lone-parent families as a proporiton of total number of census families.

[e] A "very poor neighbourhood" is defined as school being in a census tract or subdivision in which the LICO poverty rate exceeds twice the national average of 16.3 percent.

Sources: Author's calculations from FSA data provided by the BC Department of Education; data for school neighbourhood caharcteristics are from the 1996 Census.

The first variable of interest is neighbourhood family income (Table 4.3, column 4). Average neighbourhood family incomes are somewhat lower for schools with lower Aboriginal performance, suggesting that family income matters to some extent. Although families that value education can be found at all income levels, family income can influence children's education attainment through a number of routes. First, poor families often have more humble expectations for their children's careers and hence place less emphasis on their academic performance. Second, even if individual parents have high academic expectations, peer pressure can spread the low expectations of poor families through a school population. Third, wealthier parents are likely to monitor school teaching quality more aggressively than do parents of poor families. If parental monitoring matters, schools in wealthier neighbourhoods may recruit better teachers and, in general, perform better.

Neighbourhood poverty rates — by definition, the fraction of families in a neighbourhood with incomes below a defined threshold — are another potentially relevant variable (Table 4.3, column 5). Since the income effects on education are particularly acute for low-income families and since Aboriginal incomes are, on average, lower than non-Aboriginal incomes, a high overall neighbourhood poverty rate implies an even higher poverty rate among the neighbourhood's Aboriginal families.

Column 6 of Table 4.3 gives the average incidence of single-parenthood for each of the school groupings. Whether poor or not, parents without partners typically face more demands on their time than do parents with partners who share in the tasks of earning income and parenting. Single parents typically have less time to devote to helping children with their homework or participating in school affairs. Column 7 offers some data on parental education levels, the significance of which is that the children of parents who have achieved a reasonable level of education may, for various reasons, be more likely to succeed at school. Such parents may be more effective in monitoring school performance, more able to help with homework, and so on.

In the final column of Table 4.3 is the probability that a school is located in a very poor neighbourhood. Many urban analysts emphasize the idea of a neighbourhood "tipping point." The concern is that, in very poor neighbourhoods, adverse socio-economic factors are likely to interact and to have a cumulative effect that is larger than simple addition would imply. Poverty, low education, single-parenthood, high concentrations of culturally marginalized groups, and a culture of welfare dependency may combine to "tip" a neigh-bourhood into ghetto-like status. One of the adverse outcomes of a poor neighbourhood is likely to be poor school results. Not only are parents less likely to monitor school outcomes of their children, it may be particularly difficult in such neighbourhoods to organize effective teams of teachers. A proxy for this tipping point effect is a neighbourhood poverty rate that exceeds some threshold — in this case, a 1995 neighbourhood poverty rate that was more than twice the national average of 16.3 percent. Nearly one in six of the bottom quarter of schools, in terms of Aboriginal school meet/exceed scores, is in such a neighbourhood, but no school in the top quarter is so situated.

Besides neighbourhood characteristics, it is also worth consid-ering the ethnic composition of the 391 mixed BC schools. There is evidence that schools with large minority racial cohorts have problems with academic performance — one reason is that good teachers are hard for weaker schools to retain. In the United States, for example, some of the weakest schools are in inner-city neigh-bourhoods with high African American and Hispanic populations, and something analogous may be taking place in Canadian schools with proportionately large Aboriginal student cohorts. If this dynamic matters, Aboriginal student performance may be inversely related to their share of the student population. Consistent with such a story, the share of Aboriginal students in poorly performing schools is roughly twice that in schools that are performing well in terms of Aboriginal FSA scores (see Table 4.3, column 3).

Finally, Aboriginal students appear to perform better in schools that achieve better non-Aboriginal test scores (see column 2), perhaps due in part to peer pressure from non-Aboriginal students. In the

end, although neighbourhood characteristics and in-school dynamics
matter, there is much uncertainty as to the importance of the various factors that influence the academic performance of children.[16]

Policy Goals and Alternative Strategies

Improving Aboriginal education is not a simple exercise. It entails
tradeoffs among multiple goals that are rarely stated explicitly or
in a way that encourages consideration of the tradeoffs.

The Goals of Aboriginal Education Policy

In an earlier C.D. Howe Institute study, my colleague Aidan Vining
and I attempted to summarize the literature evaluating education
reforms, in the United States and Canada, intended to improve
educational achievement among minority ethnic communities (see
Richards and Vining 2004). We summarized by posing a number of
implicit goals and policy alternatives.

Enhance Aboriginal Academic Achievement

The most important goal is to enhance student academic achievement. Three distinct aspects of achievement matter when considering
any policy option: its potential effect on the performance of students
with weak academic records, many of them in poor neighbourhoods;

---

16 My colleague Aidan Vining and I undertook a preliminary regression analysis
   to assess the relative importance of variables (see Richards and Vining 2004, 14,
   25). Attempting to explain Aboriginal FSA scores using overall neighbourhood
   characteristics, it turns out, does not take us far. The regressions provide fairly
   strong evidence that FSA results decline, for both Aboriginal and non-
   Aboriginal students, as the Aboriginal share of the student population rises in
   any school. The most important single variable, in terms of its ability to
   explain the variation in Aboriginal outcomes across schools, is the school non-
   Aboriginal meet/exceed score, which supports the thesis that a rising tide lifts all
   boats. As a school improves, students tend to rise academically as an overall
   group, independent of race.

its effect on the performance of average students, mostly in non-poor neighbourhoods; and its effect on the student dropout rate.

Contain School Program Costs

A second goal is to contain school program costs. This is not to deny resources to Aboriginal schooling, but recent research (see, for example, Hanushek 2002) suggests that the link between extra resources and improved education outcomes is weak — one cannot improve outcomes simply by spending more money.

Minimize Interracial Division

Attempts to focus on improving education outcomes for Aboriginals, rather than for all students, could exacerbate interracial jealousies. Any policies should thus seek to minimize tensions and promote reconciliation.

Enable Parental Choice

The idea that all local children should attend the neighbourhood public school is intimately bound up with the rationale for public financing of education. It expresses important ideals: equal education opportunities for all children, independent of parents' incomes and social standing; the imparting to children of tolerance for social and ethnic differences; the imbibing by children of the values necessary for a sense of shared citizenship. For many, the goal of ensuring that local children attend the neighbourhood public school is second in importance only to educational achievement *per se*. There is, however, incontrovertible evidence that some neighbourhood schools, especially in poor areas, perform inadequately. What are we to do about them?

One possible policy response is to encourage parental choice. The idea of "parental choice" could be as modest as permitting parents to send their children anywhere within the school district, rather than having to attend the public school in their local catchment area. Parental choice might mean enabling multiple publicly funded school systems within the same community. More controversially, it might entail giving parents vouchers with which to buy education services from any public or private schools they choose.

An argument for choice is that parents are the best judges of their children's interests, and as such should have the right to choose which school their children attend. If parents chose good schools and shunned bad ones, it would benefit their own children and might encourage improvements in the overall quality of all schools.

Those who oppose choice raise concerns about equity. Prosperous, well-educated parents would make sure their children attended good schools, many of them private. Such parents likely would abandon their interest in neighbourhood public schools, leaving them to be monitored by less-educated, poorer parents who typically are less interested in education quality and less able to lobby school boards effectively over quality. The result, critics say, could be a downward spiral for public schools in poor neighbourhoods, and there is evidence to suggest that this fear is not groundless — see, for example, Ladd and Fiske (2001); Weiher and Tedin (2002).

Given these problems, it is naïve to analyze Aboriginal school reform without acknowledging the tension between the education ideals promoted by partisans of parental choice and those of believers in the neighbourhood school for all local children.

Minimize the Institutional Complexity of Reform

Institutional complexity raises at least two problems. First, the more complex is the proposed education reorganization, the more likely it is that some unexpected event will intervene to confound expectations. Second, the more complex is the proposed school reorganization, the more it entails disruption of established interest groups and the less likely it is to be fully implemented. Holding other things equal, even though they often are not, incremental reform is both more feasible and preferable.

Policy Alternatives for Aboriginal Education Reform

Throughout the twentieth century, black Americans migrated in large numbers from farms and villages to live and work in urban America, hoping to build better lives for themselves and their families. Mexicans cross the Rio Grande in search of the same goal. Migration is usually rational: in general, those who migrate improve their situation. But life in cities is far from perfect.

Among the problems ethnic minorities have faced in urban America is the quality of their children's education. For the past half-century, US education leaders have striven to close the education outcome gap between the children of new migrants and those of well-established urban Americans. There has been some success: many US school districts have improved outcomes, and the scores of black and white students on tests of core curriculum performance have converged somewhat. Cook and Evans (2000, 749) conclude that "nearly 75% of the convergence is due to changes within schools, that is, to a narrowing in the gap in test scores between white and black students with the same level of parental education and who attend the same school." Cook and Evans note an important problem, however: black students increasingly are found in schools of lower quality. To the extent this is so, the explanation appears to be some combination of neighbourhood residential segregation by race and income, and abandonment of the public school system by many middle-class urban parents.

The Canadian analogue to the US experience of large-scale migration of ethnic minorities has been the migration of Aboriginals from rural communities, both on- and off-reserve, to cities. One-half of all Aboriginals now live in a city and, as noted above, the great majority of Aboriginal children attend off-reserve schools run by their province, not a band-run school on-reserve. Like black and Mexican minorities in US cities, Canada's urban Aboriginals live disproportionately in poor neighbourhoods and their children attend schools whose academic outcomes are, in general, below those in more affluent neighbourhoods.

Vining and I defined the following four policy alternatives:

- *Create separate schools*: enable Aboriginals within a community to create autonomous school authorities and control public funds for some public schools in the community.
- *Enhance student mobility*: enable Aboriginals to attend good schools that already exist by eliminating limits to mobility posed by school catchment boundaries, and perhaps subsidize mobility as well.
- *Designate magnet schools*: designate one or more schools within a school district that will concentrate on Aboriginal cultural studies.
- *Enrich certain schools*: provide additional resources to improve the performance of schools with proportionately large Aboriginal student populations.

Table 4.4 summarizes our assessment of these four strategies; here, in more detail, are our conclusions.

The "Separate School" Alternative

Given the concentration of Aboriginal students in relatively weak schools, some argue for an Aboriginal school system that engages Aboriginal families more intimately and makes more extensive use of Aboriginal culture in the school curriculum. Such schools would attempt to replicate in an urban environment what former Saskatchewan premier Allan Blakeney has termed the "cultural comfort" of the reserve:

> I see it as next to impossible for us to be able to create reserves which provide an appropriate economic base for all or most of the growing population of Aboriginal people. We know that some will wish to remain [on-reserve]....We know that some will move to the cities and integrate with the economic mainstream. We know that some will move back and forth — a transitional group

....[Aboriginals] leave the reserve because there is no economic opportunity for them and particularly for their children. It seems to me that they return to the reserve because on the reserve they experience a sense of place...and also because on the reserve they have a level of cultural comfort. (Quoted in Richards 2001, 24–25.)

There is evidence to suggest that "separate schools" controlled by cultural minorities do increase educational attainment among their children (see Evans and Schwab 1995; Neal 1997). Inspired by the precedent in many provinces of distinct public school systems based on the attributes of language and religion, Blakeney has informally broached the idea of an Aboriginal-based system in cities with large Aboriginal communities.

Administratively the most complex of the four alternatives, the establishment of separate schools would explicitly challenge the ideal of the universal neighbourhood school. Such Aboriginal-controlled schools are unlikely, however, to be a panacea for urban Aboriginals hoping to preserve their cultural distinctiveness. The analogous establishment of autonomous francophone school boards in communities outside Quebec has not guaranteed the preservation of French-language use in those areas. Nevertheless, the greater engagement of Aboriginal parents and the provision of "cultural comfort" in a separate school system would probably improve the academic performance of weak students and lower their dropout rates. A separate Aboriginal school system might also create a group of Aboriginal leaders with a stake in the success of urban, as opposed to reserve-based, Aboriginal communities. One potential drawback is the danger that separate schools develop a reputation for low standards — we already know that schools with large numbers of Aboriginal students do not, in general, enjoy high academic standards.

Any province that considers undertaking the "separate school" approach should impose clear guidelines in order to minimize potential problems. The conditions that seem most important are as follows:

Table 4.4 Policy Alternatives for Aboriginal Education Reform

Goals	Alternative 1: "Separate Schools"	Alternative 2: Student Mobility	Alternative 3: Magnet School	Alternative 4: School Enrichment
Enhancing academic achievement				
Effect on students in poor neighbourhoods	potential to increase aboriginal parental involvement; probably positive effect	modestly positive effect (based on evaluation of US school-choice experiments)	positive cultural aspect might benefit low-achieving students from poor neighbourhoods	small but not trivial; subject to Hawthorne effect; innovations must be evaluated
Effect on students in typical neighbourhoods	small or no effect	negligible, provided migrating students are small share of receiving school	uncertain result, much depends on relative quality of magnet, neighbourhood schools	as above
Effect on dropout rate	potential to reduce	small impact	cultural aspect might help lower rate among low-achieving students	as above
Lowering school program costs	highest incremental costs, requires administrative duplication	medium incremental costs, much depends on premium for migrating students	low incremental costs, requires staffing or more magnet school	low-to-medium incremental costs, depending on scope of enrichment programs

Table 4.4 - continued

Goals	Alternative 1: "Separate Schools"	Alternative 2: Student Mobility	Alternative 3: Magnet School	Alternative 4: School Enrichment
Minimizing interracial cleavage	potential to improve interracial relations in medium term; potential for short-term conflicts over access to financial resources and perceived threat to racially integrated schools	may provoke non-Aboriginal opposition	as with "separate school" model	little effect
Enabling parental choice	significant increase in school choice for aboriginal parents	as with "separate school" model	provides school choice for students who gain access	no change from status quo
Minimizing administrative complexity of reform	entails major administrative adjustments	few administrative problems; many precedents exist	more complexity than alternative 2, less than alternative 1	minor adminsitrative problems

- Both Aboriginal and non-Aboriginal parents should be free to choose to send their children to either an Aboriginal school or a conventional school.
- An Aboriginal school authority should be democratically elected by all parents, including non-Aboriginal parents, with children in the system.
- To maintain standards, all schools should be required to teach the provincially mandated core curriculum, and all students should sit province-wide exams in core subjects.
- School administrations must be shielded from political pressures that may arise to lower standards.

Similar conditions have been important for the successful coexistence of Catholic and nondenominational public school systems and for systems based on one or other of the two official languages. The fourth point raises the requirement that any urban Aboriginal school authority must address outcomes. Pressure to avoid outcome measurement would not be unique to this model of Aboriginal-run schools. But the need to resist such pressure and establish educational legitimacy would be greater for such schools, particularly in the short term.

Enhancing Student Mobility

Student mobility is of particular relevance for parents who want to avoid sending their children to poorly performing schools. A choice of schools is usually not feasible in rural areas, where schools are widely dispersed, but is an option for the increasing numbers of Aboriginals living in urban areas.

One of the best-known and most radical experiments in school choice has been under way in Milwaukee, Wisconsin, since 1990. Targeted at families whose incomes are less than 175 percent of the designated poverty line, the state-funded Milwaukee program offers vouchers that enable students to attend private schools — worth US$4,700 per student in the 1997–98 school year. The number of vouchers is limited and students are selected randomly from eligible applicants. In a survey of this and similar experiments, Sawhill and Smith (2000) conclude that results are "modestly encouraging." They note, however, the mixed evidence that the Milwaukee experiment improves student achievement:

> One study, by Paul Peterson and his colleagues, found that by the third and fourth year of the program, [students in the program] had made sizable gains relative to their public school counterparts in both reading and math. Another study, by John Witte and his colleagues, found no differences between the two groups. And a third study, by Cecilia Rouse, found gains in math but not in reading. There are several reasons for these differences, including how each research team selected its control or comparison group and how they chose to adjust for any remaining differences between students who took advantage of the voucher and those who remained in the Milwaukee public schools. After carefully reviewing these three studies, we conclude that...it is simply not possible at the current time to render a clear verdict on the outcomes of the experiment. (274–75.)[17]

The evidence suggests, at worst, that the experiment has made no difference.

There is, however, support for the claim that enabling modest levels of competition between schools and between school districts — reforms less radical than the Milwaukee voucher scheme — does improve school outcomes.[18] Cowley and Easton (2004, 3) enthusiastically argue that "all Aboriginal parents should have the unfettered right to enroll their children in any school that they choose." Vining and I also defend the expansion of school choice, although with more qualifications. One modest parental choice model that could improve Aboriginal school outcomes is to let Aboriginal parents send their children to any school in the school district, rather

---

17 For access to the three studies of the Milwaukee school choice experiment mentioned in this quotation, see Greene, Peterson, and Du (1996); Rouse (1998); and Witte (2000).

18 See, for example, Borland and Howsen (1992); Zanzig (1997); Bishop (2000).

than be restricted by school catchment boundaries — a reform rendered more feasible by recent legislation in British Columbia.

With the passing of the *School Amendment Act, 2002*,[19] BC parents can now choose to send their children to any public school in the province — if they can find the space. Children within the school's catchment area have first priority, and how much space to make available to students beyond the catchment area is up to the school district, a discretion that weakens the effect of the reform for all students. Despite that weakness, the act seems to have had some impact within the Vancouver school district, where Steffenhagen (2003) finds informal evidence that parents are choosing schools that perform better on test scores.

Any strategy involving choice should include appropriate incentives for good schools to accept Aboriginal students, perhaps including paying them a "mobility bonus" for the number of migrating children they accept. School boards anxious to avoid explicit racial targeting could make such a bonus contingent on income, as is the case in the Milwaukee experiment.

The mobility alternative would primarily benefit Aboriginal parents who are conscious of the value of academically good schools and willing to incur the costs of sending their children to such a school even if it is not in the neighbourhood. This reform would be much less administratively complex than the "separate school" option and less controversial than school vouchers.

Designating Magnet Schools

A "magnet" school — also called a "charter" school — is a tax-funded school within a public school system that enjoys a "charter" allowing it to specialize in a particular field of study. Any student in the school district can elect to attend the school, subject to its capacity.

An interesting Canadian example of a magnet school is Amiskwaciy Academy.[20] A secondary school in the Edmonton school

---

19 For a summary of the act's provisions, see Internet web site: http://www.bced.gov.bc.ca/legislation/legp502.htm.

20 See the academy's Internet web site: http://amiskwaciy.epsb.net.

district, it has a mandate to specialize in Aboriginal cultural studies. It follows the same core curriculum as other Alberta schools, but supplemented with courses on Aboriginal history, literature, and culture. All students who live in Edmonton, whether Aboriginal or not, are eligible to attend.

In terms of meeting the goals laid out earlier, magnet schools offer a compromise between the school enrichment and separate school alternatives. It allows for schools that explicitly encourage Aboriginal studies and concerns, without the administrative complexity that would accompany the establishing of a separate school authority.

Enriching Certain Schools

A fourth strategy is for governments to provide additional resources to schools with large Aboriginal student contingents. The BC government already includes the number of Aboriginal students in determining the funding formula for school boards, and the Vancouver board provides such schools in its district with extra library resources bearing on Aboriginal literature, arts, and history. School boards may also supplement the budgets of these schools to engage Aboriginal elders as counselors and to hire highly motivated teachers. The strategy could be extended to include early childhood education programs, attached to particular schools and targeted to attract Aboriginal children.

A weakness of such a strategy is that it relies exclusively on the supply side to improve school quality. The three previous alternatives, in contrast, invoke parental choice as, in effect, a demand-side check on quality in addition to the checks made by school authorities themselves. A separate Aboriginal school system would enable parents to choose between systems; enhanced mobility would add more choices for Aboriginal parents in urban school districts and could offer financial payments to recipient schools; and magnet schools also promise some degree of choice.

Another potential problem with enriching certain schools is the "Hawthorne effect" — the frequently observed phenomenon that short-term results improve immediately following an experimental intervention, regardless of the nature of the intervention. The immediate improvement may have more to do with the change in routines and increased attention paid by supervisors than with the efficacy of the reform itself, the determination of which would require a longer-term evaluation.

Conclusion

Any school board prepared to tackle Aboriginal education reform aggressively should probably have as its agenda a combination of the second, third, and fourth alternatives discussed above — namely:

- relaxation of neighbourhood school boundaries and payment of a financial bonus to schools to encourage them to accept Aboriginal students who migrate from beyond the relevant school catchment area;
- in large urban communities, creation of one or more magnet schools concentrating on Aboriginal cultural studies; and
- provision of generous enrichment programs for schools with large Aboriginal student populations.

It is probably more important to experiment actively than to seek the single optimum strategy. Edmonton, for example, is undertaking a natural experiment. While the city's nondenominational public school board is pursuing a magnet schools strategy, its Catholic school board has chosen the school enrichment approach. In a survey, the great majority of Aboriginal parents of children in the Catholic system expressed a preference for Aboriginal content within neighbourhood schools that otherwise remained integrated with non-Aboriginal students. In response, the Catholic board has embarked on an ambitious program to enrich Aboriginal content in schools with sizable Aboriginal student populations; the program includes hiring Aboriginal teachers and involving elders in schools (Sparklingeyes 2005).

Beyond these specific recommendations is the matter of political priorities. Realizing the convergence of education outcomes will require a more consistent commitment to Aboriginal education success on the part of all concerned. This means a commitment by Aboriginal leaders and federal and provincial politicians on targets. Realizing targets requires, in turn, detailed benchmarking of the status quo (as British Columbia is doing via the FSA), a willingness to experiment (as, for example, is happening in Edmonton), and evaluation of outcomes (which, as the Auditor General notes with respect to on-reserve schools, Ottawa and band councils are not doing).

When the prime minister, premiers, and leaders of the major Aboriginal organizations met in Kelowna, BC, in late 2005, they agreed to address social problems and not to debate disagreements among themselves over the respective powers to be exercised by Ottawa, the provinces, and band governments. With respect to education, they committed themselves to "the goal of closing the gap in K–12 educational attainment between Aboriginal learners and other Canadians by 2016" (Canada 2005d, 4). It is highly unlikely they will realize this goal, but stating it is worthwhile — for at least two reasons.

First, this is an implicit acknowledgment by the prime minister and Aboriginal leaders that past education performance by both the Department of Indian Affairs and band councils has been woefully inadequate. It is also an acknowledgment by the premiers that their provincial education ministries must assume major responsibilities with respect to improving Aboriginal education, and that they can no longer sidestep the difficulties by reference to federal or band responsibility.

Second, it is in the nature of organizations to pursue goals that are explicitly stated. Having stated the target of eliminating the Aboriginal–non-Aboriginal gap in K–12 education levels, national leaders have almost certainly set in motion an invigorated dynamic to improve education outcomes. An initial result will probably be more adequate documentation of the current gap between Aboriginal and non-Aboriginal education levels. Those interested can cite this commitment in order to obtain evidence with respect to the size of the gap among Aboriginal children living on- and off-reserve, with respect to the size of the gap among children across provinces, across school districts within a province, and finally across individual schools within a school district.

As I have noted, it is highly unlikely that the K–12 education gap will be closed by 2016. A skeptic might ask whether it will ever be closed. One reason for skepticism — there are others — is to ask how serious the reserve-based Aboriginal leadership is about realizing social policy goals, such as closing the education gap, that ignore the agenda of treaty rights and blur the distinction between Aboriginals living on- or off-reserve. In the next chapter, I turn to the delicate subject of defining appropriate limits to the agenda of Aboriginal nationalism.

5 *Defining Limits*

The civil rights movement among African Americans in the two decades following World War II; the Quiet Revolution among francophone Quebecers (whom I refer to for convenience as "Québécois") in the 1960s and 1970s; the claim among North American Aboriginals over the last decades of the twentieth century to an expansive reinterpretation of their rights as descendants of the indigenous population. Here are three prominent examples of North American mass movements among minorities.

Each of the three minorities displays marked differences in culture and/or ethnicity from the North American majority. Historically, the majority had, to varying degrees, marginalized all three groups and treated them as inferior. And, incontestably, most members of these groups have benefited from the movements. In each case, the movement had an element of spontaneity, taking off in a manner few, even those centrally engaged as leaders, could have expected. Nor did many predict the various stages through which the majority response would evolve: from initial indifference to the minority's grievances, through acknowledgment of past wrongs and search for accommodation, to skepticism and a wish to define limits.

The spontaneous enthusiasm of the first generation of a mass movement cannot readily be sustained. Over time, movements launch organized political parties or political lobbies and define explicit goals entailing political power and/or fiscal benefits for the group — secession and the formation of an independent state, for example. Given certain prerequisites — a region of reasonable size within which the minority comprise the majority, a reasonably productive regional economy, coherent political leadership, and a non-violent political response by the majority — secession can succeed, as we have seen with the creation of many newly independent states since the demise of the Soviet Empire.

Of the three North American examples, only the Québécois have been in a position to form a viable new state. They form the majority within a well-defined territory having a productive economy; they have formed successful political organizations with sovereignty as the goal, and they have faced a non-bellicose majority outside Quebec. African Americans and Aboriginals, however, are geographically dispersed. Unlike Quebec for the Québécois, any region in which these groups comprise the majority — say, Canada's northern territories in the case of Aboriginals — is home to only a small share of the group's total population. Such isolated regions also cannot generate per capita incomes comparable to those prevailing elsewhere in North America. Moreover, African American and Aboriginal communities are inextricably intertwined with other ethnic communities — even in the case of Quebec, the intermingling of English- and French-speaking communities in the Ottawa Valley and in Montreal might confound any project for secession with existing borders.

If nationalist movements do not — or cannot — realize secession, then what? There is a wide range of possibilities from international experience. The movement may remain a simple matter of cultural advocacy, as with Bretons within a French state that has few traditions of accommodating national minorities. As with Irish republicans in Ulster or *autonomistes* in Corsica, factions within the movement may undertake debilitating vigilante violence that inspires tit-for-tat violence by opponents. Vigilante violence may escalate into civil war, as in Sri Lanka, where the Tamil minority and Sinhalese majority have waged intermittent war for two decades. Or the central authorities may accept a federal-type devolution of power in an attempt to lower the secessionist appeal, as in Scotland and Catalonia.

Canadians are the world's most enthusiastic advocates of federalism, but it is not a panacea. It succeeded in maintaining Czechs and Slovaks within a single country for many decades, but their federation did not survive the turmoil following the demise of the Soviet Empire. Yugoslavia did not survive the death of Tito, without whose tactical skill at accommodation and adroit use of force Serb nationalists precipitated civil war and dismemberment of the federation. It is not certain that "federalizing" Belgium will preserve the unity of that country.

The rise of Aboriginal nationalism has been accompanied by occasional acts of violence over the past three decades: conflict over use of land at Oka, Quebec, and Gustafson Lake, British Columbia, for example, or the shooting by police of an Aboriginal at Ipperwash, Ontario, and the dumping of Aboriginals by police on the roadside outside Saskatoon in the dead of winter. But these acts are exceptions in what has been an intense but largely peaceful political undertaking. In general, Aboriginal nationalism has served as a set of ideas, an ideology enabling Aboriginal leaders to make their case: first, to mobilize Aboriginals and, second, to persuade non-Aboriginals of the justice of their political demands.

Both uses of Aboriginal nationalism underlie its success. Without the support of the majority of Aboriginals — both status Indians and others — the language of treaty rights would lack legitimacy. Of equal importance, success has required convincing the non-Aboriginal majority that the policies in place prior to Trudeau's White Paper had been racist, and that the White Paper's goal of integration was itself misguided if not racist.

The progress of Aboriginal nationalism is evident on many fronts. Historical treaties were brief documents and their wording was often ambiguous. Since the entrenchment of "existing Aboriginal and treaty rights" in section 35 of the *Constitution Act, 1982*, Aboriginal leaders have won numerous legal battles to establish broad interpretations of treaties. They have also persuaded federal politicians to make large, seemingly permanent fiscal transfers to band councils that, cumulatively, now approach $6 billion out of a total of $9 billion in annual federal expenditures on services to Aboriginals. And Aboriginal leaders have persuaded politicians, both provincial and federal, to negotiate generous new treaties and agreements that provide for substantial political autonomy to band councils and for rights of Aboriginal access to land and natural resources.

Limits to Nationalism: The Quebec Example

Earlier, I referred to Shelby Steele's (2002) dichotomy of white American attitudes toward blacks: the idea of racial superiority that was dominant from the beginning of the slave economy in the sixteenth century to the civil rights movement of the mid-twentieth century, and the feeling of "white guilt" that has now replaced it. One can apply Steele's idea more generally. Often, when a prosperous majority assesses a marginalized cultural minority, its initial reaction is one of superiority combined with various notions of inherent racial ranking. In response, leaders among the minority face two tasks: to mobilize their own community and simultaneously to persuade the majority to recant.

A characteristic of emerging nationalist movements is to put forward new explanations of their marginal status. Why have members of the group suffered? Why are they poorer, less well educated, less politically influential than others? Explanations may entail an element of self-criticism: in the mid-twentieth century, leaders of Quebec's Quiet Revolution criticized the excesses of piety and lack of attention to technical and professional education on the part of the Roman Catholic hierarchy that, at the time, played a large role in provincial politics and dominated education policy. Invariably, however, nationalist movements place much of the blame for the group's marginal status on sins of omission and commission by outsiders. Many Québécois nationalists portrayed the Catholic hierarchy and provincial politicians of those days as quasi-colonial administrators who were accommodating an anglo-Canadian elite that, ever since *la Conquête,* had preserved key decisions to itself.

One must be careful here. To blame outsiders and excuse one's supporters is a common denominator of political discourse. To observe that political leaders indulge in such practices establishes neither the truth nor falseness of a political argument. Often, nationalist explanations of events falsify or seriously distort history. Sometimes, they come as close to truth as is possible given the ambiguities of historical explanation. And the solutions they propose may or may not be accepted as reasonable by those who stand to bear the costs of their implementation.

What Does Quebec Want?
What Does Canada Want?

In the early years of Quebec's Quiet Revolution, most Canadians outside Quebec (whom I shall label anglo-Canadians for convenience) were supportive. Québécois novelists, playwrights, and singers became famous across Canada. Canadians expected an energetic provincial government, led by Jean Lesage, to modernize the province's social services and infrastructure. Initially, anglo-Canadians ignored the tensions between the Québécois nationalism of Lesage's supporters and the pan-Canadian nationalism implicit among Trudeau's. However, Lesage's "*maître chez nous*" evolved into René Lévesque's "*souveraineté-association*" and anglo-Canadian sympathy waned. "What does Quebec want?" was posed in the 1970s with less empathy than in the previous decade. By 1990, the year the Meech Lake Accord collapsed, the dominant anglo-Canadian attitude had become one of skepticism toward the constitutional demands of Quebec nationalists, whether they be federalists in the Quebec Liberal Party or sovereignists in the Parti Québécois.

Underlying much of the Quebec–Canada conflict since the 1960s has been the matter of language policy. The lowest common denominator, on which virtually all Québécois agree, is that French should survive as the common language of the province and that it not succumb to folkloric status, as has been the fate of all languages, other than English and Spanish, that immigrants have brought to North America.

Before 1960, Quebec was much more homogeneously of French origin than the rest of Canada was British. An element of the secular, modernizing government of Jean Lesage was to welcome immigration. Like Toronto and Vancouver, Montreal has become a multicultural city. At the same time, Montreal is the only metropolitan centre in North America that produces works of high art and mass culture, sustains major universities, and conducts sophisticated business in French, and Québécois elites have insisted that French continue to be the dominant language in Montreal for most of these public purposes.

In the 1960s and 1970s, the realization of this goal was problematic. Immigration was increasing the share of allophones (those whose mother tongue was neither French nor English) in the population. The new immigrants felt little loyalty to Quebec's francophone history — they were neighbours to a small group of six million francophones but, quite reasonably, identified as part of a continent of 300 million anglophones. Allophones were making a rational cost-benefit choice and, in a ratio approaching ten to one, were opting for English over French as medium of instruction for their children.

The linguistic implication was obvious; so too, among the great majority of the francophone elite, was the solution: protection for the French language. A decade of political debate culminated in the adoption of *La Charte de la langue française* — the law better known as Bill 101, the number attached to the draft legislation as Camille Laurin shepherded it through the National Assembly in 1977. Thereby, Quebec adopted a language regime similar to that prevailing in small European countries whose languages are overshadowed by those of large neighbours.

Opponents of Bill 101 — Pierre Trudeau prominent among them — condemned the restrictions placed on free linguistic choice between English and French within Quebec public institutions. Ottawa's policy of official bilingualism, in contrast, promoted French within the federal bureaucracy and minority language rights for French- and English-speakers across Canada, through both legislation and entrenchment of official language minority rights in the Charter of Rights and Freedoms. Official bilingualism did not, however, address the core problem, as the Québécois saw it: the preservation of franco-phone predominance in Montreal.

The clash between the logic of Bill 101 and that of the Charter of Rights reached a crescendo in the furor surrounding the Supreme Court of Canada's 1988 *Ford* decision on language for commercial signs. Presumably realizing the decision's affront to Québécois sensibilities, the Supreme Court delayed its release until after the hotly contested election on free trade held that year. In *Ford*, the Court gave broad interpretation to the free speech provision of the Charter (and Quebec's human rights legislation) and struck down Bill 101's provision specifying unilingual French commercial signs.

Read literally, the decision did not change much of substance in Quebec's language regime. As precedent, it changed a great deal. It implied that the Supreme Court of Canada, an institution dominated by anglophones, would be the final arbiter as to when and how Québécois could exercise linguistic protection. *Ford* catalyzed Quebec nationalist opinion and revived political support for the separatist Parti Québécois. Under intense public pressure to respond to the decision, the provincial Liberal government of Robert Bourassa used the Charter's notwithstanding clause to impose a legislated compromise.

Between the first election of a Parti Québécois government in 1976 and today lie three decades of constitutional uncertainty. *Ford* and its aftermath comprise only one, albeit important, chapter in this saga. The decision itself excited passions among Québécois, as did Quebec's use of the notwithstanding clause in response among non-francophones in Quebec and the majority elsewhere in Canada. The immediate victim of these conflicting passions was the Meech Lake Accord.

Canada and Quebec Today

In any assessment of Quebec nationalism, the past decade can be summarized as the decade in which limits were set. Not that the anglo-Canadian majority prevailed on all matters — far from it. But the Québécois were obliged to accept limits to their agenda. The narrowness of the federalist majority in the 1995 referendum induced a welcome dilution in Ottawa of Trudeau's tradition of justiciable language rights. In 2005, for example, the Supreme Court upheld Bill 101's restriction on access to English language instruction in the provincial school system (*Gosselin v Québec* 2005). If anglo-Canadian elites now accept, more or less, the legitimacy of the *Charte de la langue française*, Québécois elites must now accept that it is legitimate to ask, "what does Canada want?" The Canadian majority has defined limits: it mistrusts constitutional provisions that afford Quebec an ambiguous special status distinct from that of other provinces. Quebec may secede, subject to the constraints imposed by the *Clarity Act*, the majority agrees, and it may negotiate modest administrative arrangements that do not apply to other provinces. It will not obtain any constitutional acknowledgment of its "distinct society."

On another front, the 1990s saw initiatives to curtail the redistribution of money from Ontario and western Canada to Quebec and the four Atlantic provinces. Since the 1960s, Quebec politicians — federalist and sovereignist — had bargained aggressively over interregional transfers, posing the spectre of secession if expectations were frustrated. Unwilling, in the case of Trudeau's government, and unable, in the case of Mulroney's, to accommodate Quebec's cultural agenda, politicians in Ottawa "bought" short-term acquiescence in the status quo through redistributive policies that were particularly generous to Quebec. Atlantic Canada benefited more, on a per capita basis, from most interregional transfers than Quebec did, but the size of Quebec's population meant that it was the major beneficiary in absolute terms of several major programs whose parameters remained intact until the fiscal crisis of the 1990s (see Boothe 1998). Equalization payments, as such, were not contentious, but Quebec's privileged status with respect to the cost sharing of social assistance and unemployment insurance were major irritants in provincial capitals west of Ottawa.[1]

---

1   At their peak in the early 1990s, federal programs with interregional redistribution as an explicit goal — that is, the major intergovernmental transfers plus unemployment insurance — amounted to one-third of Ottawa's program spending.

Reconciliation between the Québécois and English-speaking Canada remains imperfect. Although the Parti Québécois is currently out of office, sovereignty continues to attract many francophones.[2] But the bitterness of earlier decades has subsided. English-speaking elites have set aside the logic of the *Ford* decision. And Quebec elites accept, more or less, the case for not returning to the regime of inter-provincial transfers that prevailed until 1995, from which Quebec benefited so disproportionately.

Implications of the Quebec Experience for Aboriginals

An obvious parallel exists between the cultural expectations of Québécois and Aboriginals. Neither group perceives itself simply as one among many immigrant communities in North America, whose fate is to dissolve in an English-speaking industrial society. Viewed with hindsight, the 1988 *Ford* decision and the 1969 White Paper on Aboriginal policy have much in common. In both instances, Ottawa elites undertook initiatives they perceived as important in order to defend the principle of equal individual rights for all Canadians. Both can be seen in retrospect as ill-advised ventures that catalyzed minority nationalist opinion in opposition to Canadian political institutions because they implied repudiation of matters of profound collective importance to the relevant minority.

What lessons from the Quebec experience, then, apply to Aboriginal policy? The obvious one is that the non-Aboriginal majority

2   In a May 2005 poll, conducted in the midst of hearings on the sponsorship scandal, 54 percent of respondents expressed support for sovereignty with an economic association with Canada. Among francophones, support was 62 percent; among anglophones, 13 percent; and among allophones, 31 percent. Independence without any economic association found the support of 46 percent of respondents, with 52 percent of francophones, 10 percent of anglophones, and 22 percent of allophones in favour. The sponsorship scandal has generated levels of support for sovereignty/independence not seen since the 1995 referendum campaign (Léger and Léger 2005).

needs to accept the legitimacy of institutions that enable Aboriginal culture to survive from one generation to the next. Primarily, this means ensuring the survival of reserves as viable communities and adding Aboriginal cultural content to provincial school curricula.

A second lesson, which Aboriginal leaders should heed, is that, in the coming years, the majority will question the efficacy of the large transfers that the Department of Indian Affairs makes to band councils. Among band leaders, Ottawa's fiscal transfers are interpreted as a treaty right, as partial compensation for lands expropriated. Moreover, in their view, the principle of Aboriginal self-government precludes close oversight by Parliament or provincial legislatures in band administration. The non-Aboriginal majority, however, increasingly perceives the current level of accountability as inadequate.

Limits to Welfare Dependency: The US Example

With the formal end to slavery in the United States in the 1860s, slaves became farmers, most of them sharecroppers who did not own their own land. Over the first half of the twentieth century, a vast rural-to-urban migration took place. As part of that migration, the children and grandchildren of ex-slaves abandoned rural life in search of higher incomes and better education for their children in the country's growing industrial cities. A dense network of racial policies and prejudice obliged many black urban Americans to live in segregated neighbourhoods.

Black reformers of the mid-twentieth century were particularly concerned with fighting segregationist laws and regulations, but they also advocated expansion of social programs for low-income Americans. Federal, state, and municipal governments responded with, among other things, funding for large public housing projects, health insurance benefits under the Medicaid program, and other social programs. One such program, Aid to Families with Dependent Children (AFDC), begun as a minor New Deal program intended primarily for widows with children, became by the 1960s the major source of funds for state-provided social assistance. A disproportionate share of the beneficiaries of public housing, AFDC, and Medicaid were African American.

In combination, such programs generated an unexpected phenomenon: the growth of large urban neighbourhoods of concentrated intergenerational poverty.[3] When legal barriers to residential integration began to topple in the years following World War II, the black middle class moved "uptown." Poor black neighbourhoods lost many of their more affluent community leaders, who no longer needed to live in low-income neighbourhoods. Among the poor who remained in these neighbourhoods, a syndrome of overlapping problems intensified. Public housing projects constrained residential mobility. Low-quality schools in ghetto neighbourhoods assured intergenerational continuity of low education levels. The fiscal incentives implicit in AFDC, Medicaid, and eligibility rules for public housing projects discouraged employment and the formation of stable, two-parent families. Often, full-time employment at wages available to those with low skills afforded less income (in cash and in kind) than did social programs. Low levels of employment among young men encouraged crime, which accelerated residential segregation by income as middle-class people — of all races — chose to live elsewhere.

In the 1970s and 1980s, a more conservative judiciary began to set limits on the expectations of the civil rights era of the 1960s. Affirmative action programs came under review, and many cities — most notably New York — attempted to restore civic norms in ghetto neighbourhoods by more aggressive policing of street crime. Most significantly, starting with major negative income tax experiments in the 1970s, Americans have engaged in a controversial rethinking of welfare policy. Many states, such as Wisconsin, now link eligibility for benefits to work and training obligations, and the

3 For further reading, see Moffitt (2003). Elsewhere (Richards 2001), I have written a survey of US anti-poverty policy with an emphasis on changing ideas about welfare in the context of urban ghettos.

largest single anti-poverty program Washington now funds is the Earned Income Tax Credit, an "in-work" benefit to low-income families with children.[4]

The symbolic climax to the US debate over welfare policy came in 1996 with a reform bill that put an end to AFDC and invented a new block grant to states called Temporary Assistance to Needy Families. Under the new rules, states were given wide discretion over the design of their welfare programs with few of Washington's strings attached. Leaders of the black community — the group that would be most affected by the reform bill — and many liberals in the New Deal tradition urged then-president Bill Clinton to veto the bill. He did not. Since then, the results have in general vindicated the bill's supporters: welfare roles have declined sharply; employment among poor, single parents has risen, and, to some extent, so have their post-tax, post-transfer incomes.

Viewed with hindsight, much of the US social policy debate over the past quarter-century has been an interracial dialogue in which the majority has set limits to the agenda of the New Deal coalition and the civil rights movement that followed. Mainstream US politicians now insist that social policy endorse the core values of the majority, one of which is that social policy distinguish between the employable and unemployable poor and that aid to the former be linked to their actively seeking employment. The exercise whereby black and white politicians have struck new social bargains has been protracted and surrounded by controversy. But interracial relations in the United States are healthier for having undertaken a blunt dialogue over the limits of intergenerational welfare dependency, a disfiguring feature of poverty in modern societies and one that has particularly afflicted African American communities.

---

4   This program is geared to earnings, not family need. For eligible families, it
    augments the wage rate by an amount, depending on family size, up to three
    dollars per hour.

Implications of the US Welfare Experience for Aboriginals

Canada's Department of Indian Affairs transfers about $6 billion a year to band councils. The councils, in turn, provide social assistance worth about $1 billion a year to 150,000 on-reserve beneficiaries. Over the past quarter-century, on average, more than 40 percent of the on-reserve population has been in receipt of social assistance. Off-reserve, between a one-quarter and one-half of welfare beneficiaries in Western Canada are Aboriginal.[5]

Except for some limited reforms in Alberta, no dialogue analogous to the US welfare reform debate has yet taken place in Canada between Aboriginal and non-Aboriginal political leaders.[6] Aware of the potentially racist excesses of any such debate, most federal and provincial political leaders have avoided the subject. The tenor of current social policy discussion, particularly in western Canada, where Aboriginals are a much more sizable component of the community, has much in common with that in the United States in the 1960s. The majority of Americans at the time endorsed the civil rights agenda that put an end to legal discrimination, but had yet to engage the complex issues surrounding low education levels and high welfare dependency among black Americans. Something analogous can be said about Canadians today with respect to Aboriginals.

---

5   The range is based on estimates by senior provincial officials; provincial social assistance agencies do not collect data on the ethnic origin of beneficiaries.

6   In 1993, Mike Cardinal, a civil-servant-turned-politician, an Aboriginal, and a consistent critic of the perverse impact of welfare on Aboriginal communities, was appointed minister of social services in Alberta. At the time, Albertans' collective reliance on social assistance was similar to that of residents of the two other Prairie provinces. Under Cardinal's direction, Alberta launched a welfare reform program that, in broad outline, resembled US state programs more than those of other Canadian provinces. The core strategy underlying the "Cardinal reforms" was the imposition of high barriers to welfare access among those deemed employable, combined with some training support and help in work placement. (See Boessenkool 1997; Richards 2005.)

Defining Limits to Aboriginal Nationalism

Relative to the Quiet Revolution in Quebec and the civil rights movement of the United States, present-day Aboriginal nationalism is a more recent phenomenon, having taken off in the 1970s. The complex political exercise whereby the majority defines limits to that nationalism has yet to be seriously engaged, but it has begun.

In 1999, in its *Marshall* decision, the Supreme Court of Canada interpreted an ambiguous mid-eighteenth-century treaty as giving Indians a broad, treaty-based fishing right. Non-Aboriginal fishermen refused to accept the legitimacy of the decision, and spontaneous vigilante violence forced the Court to qualify its decision with a lengthy addendum. On the other side of the country, non-Aboriginal opinion on the comprehensive Nisga'a Treaty in British Columbia was sharply divided. Misgiving among non-Aboriginals over the extent of the powers and money to be transferred under the treaty prompted a new provincial government to conduct a referendum in 2002 on how it should conduct future treaty negotiations.

Aboriginal leaders challenged the legitimacy of the referendum. Treaties, they insisted, were a matter of constitutionally entrenched rights and should be negotiated nation-to-nation by representatives of First Nations, Ottawa, and the province; they were not a matter subject to majoritarian sentiment among non-Aboriginals. The two key propositions of the referendum concerned the powers of Aboriginal governments and taxation. Voters were asked whether they agreed or disagreed with the statements that "Aboriginal self-government should have the characteristics of local government, with powers delegated from Canada and British Columbia" and that "The existing tax exemptions for Aboriginal people should be phased out."

In the referendum, British Columbians voted in favour of all its propositions by large majorities; Aboriginal organizations urged their supporters to boycott the vote, however, which biased the results. A more accurate snapshot of majority opinion is probably the Ipsos-Reid opinion poll conducted during the referendum campaign. It indicated majority support for the government's decision to conduct the referendum despite Aboriginal objections, and the support of three out of five respondents for the two critical propositions on the powers of Aboriginal governments and taxation.[7]

I close this chapter with an exchange of ideas between two of Canada's most prominent political scientists, Alan Cairns and Tom Flanagan. In 2000, both published, nearly simultaneously, important reviews of Aboriginal policy since the 1969 White Paper (Cairns 2000; Flanagan 2000). Both books were attempts to define appropriate limits to Aboriginal nationalism, to render it compatible with the encompassing institutions of Canadian political life. In a subsequent exchange of "letters" between the two, Flanagan concluded:

> In the case of aboriginal peoples, the political aspect of the identity seems to have enlarged as the cultural differences have shrunk. As Indians, Métis, and Inuit have become more like other people in the way they live, they have become more insistent that they are separate nations possessing an inherent right to self-government and sweeping claims to ownership of land and resources. You and I seem to agree that this approach, if interpreted literally and pushed hard, is incompatible with Canadian federalism and the larger constitutional order....
>
> [W]e lack systematic evidence about what works and what does not work in the area of band government. Why do some communities seem well administered, entrepreneurial, and fiscally responsible, while others seem prone to patronage, factional infighting, and chronic over-spending? Is it just a question of local leadership? Do cultural differences among First Nations also make a difference? Are some organizational structures more effective than others? The Hawthorn commission tried to address some of these questions in its own day, but the setting has changed radically since then. (Cairns and Flanagan 2001, 116–17.)

---

7   For a report on the poll results, see Matas and Mickleburgh (2002). On the poll question: "Overall, do you think that holding this referendum will have a positive or negative impact on treaty negotiations with BC's Aboriginal peoples over the next few years, or do you think it will have no impact at all?", 25 percent of respondents said "positive", 52 percent said "negative", and 20 percent said "no impact".

The Hawthorn Report had used the expression "citizens plus" in its major survey of Aboriginal conditions (Canada 1966–67), and Cairns had borrowed it for the title of his book. "Citizens plus," suggested Cairns, was an appropriate starting point for effecting a workable compromise:

> [T]he Aboriginal future is within Canada, for both Aboriginal peoples living in cities and those living in organized communities. This...means...that Aboriginal peoples are not only Canadians, but are and should be thought of as such by others and by themselves. This was the argument of the Hawthorn survey a third of a century ago....*Citizens Plus* is an attempt to revive the necessity and relevance of the citizen component which I see as threatened by a policy discourse that pays more attention to how we can be kept apart than to what will hold us together. My fear is that an exaggerated stress on "otherness," on incommensurable solitudes, on a multinational definition of who we are, may lead us to treat each other as strangers with little moral obligation to help each other. (Cairns and Flanagan 2001, 110–11.)

Flanagan and Cairns disagree on much, but both want to lower the social tensions that arise when minority group leaders disparage intergroup interaction on grounds of cultural differences and a history of mistrust. Apart from his insistence that many Aboriginals prefer an urban lifestyle and that Ottawa should not place all its eggs in a rural reserve-based basket, Cairns does not say much about how to reduce "an exaggerated stress on 'otherness'" and maintain a "moral obligation to help each other." Nor does Flanagan.

Flanagan poses a second reason for defining limits to the Aboriginal nationalist agenda: "[W]e lack systematic evidence about what works and what does not work in the area of band government." After three decades of optimistic anthropology and attendant institutional parallelism, there has been very little neutral evaluation of Aboriginal policy — as is evident in the Auditor General of Canada's frustration over government and band failure to evaluate the performance of on-reserve schools. In the final chapter, I venture some conclusions about what does and does not work, and propose some content to the slogan "citizens plus."

6 *Time to Rethink*

Canada cannot — nor should it — return to the pre–1969 White Paper world of pessimistic anthropology and its accompanying policies. But the current absence of limits to the Aboriginal nationalist discourse is disturbing. The stress on "otherness" among reserve-based Aboriginal leaders encourages many of them to abdicate their responsibility to assess "what works and what does not work" among on-reserve programs, and to underestimate the extent to which many Aboriginals wish to live in the mainstream of industrial society. The discourse also encourages many non-Aboriginal leaders to minimize their responsibility to assess "what works and what does not work" among off-reserve programs.

Over the past three decades, the scope for Aboriginal government envisioned by Aboriginal leaders has vastly expanded, from the municipal to something approaching sovereignty. For many, the ideal is the Nisga'a Treaty, the one modern treaty negotiated in British Columbia. This treaty, 250 pages in length, entrenches a third order of government with very large powers. As Gordon Gibson (1999, 169) summarizes,

> Because most cash and resources in the [local] economy will flow through the Nisga'a government by virtue of the terms of the

Treaty, people will be uncommonly dependent upon and beholden to that government. This dependence will not be merely for municipal-type services — roads, garbage and so on — but also for matters of intense and immediate importance to the individuals concerned, such as housing, social assistance and employment.

Defenders of current policy point to the fact that social outcomes for Aboriginals have in general improved since the 1970s. But improvements have come very slowly, and many gaps between Aboriginal and non-Aboriginal social outcomes loom as large as in the past. Whatever the ultimate root causes in past history, the key proximate variable, I suggest, is low levels of Aboriginal education. Low education induces low employment rates and the intergenerational perpetuation of poverty. In turn, low employment is linked to criminal activity and depression — among men, in particular — abuse of alcohol, a high suicide rate, and an epidemic of diabetes. To the extent that low employment matters in explaining remaining health problems, health and education outcomes are inextricably linked.

Aboriginal incomes are higher than three decades ago but remain far below those of non-Aboriginals. Educational attainment is higher among younger Aboriginals than their elder generations, which is encouraging — although a similar improvement is evident among non-Aboriginals. Yet, if Aboriginals are to earn incomes comparable to those of other Canadians, on- and off-reserve Aboriginal education levels remain seriously deficient. The evidence from 15-to-24-year-olds is not reassuring.

In thinking about pragmatic reforms, and inspired by Alan Cairns's hope that Canadians of good faith resurrect the notion of Aboriginals as "citizens plus," I pose three questions that should underlie dialogue about both the "citizen" and the "plus" components. First, what aspects of citizenship should the Aboriginal minority share with the non-Aboriginal majority? Second, what special spending and taxation powers should band councils exercise? And third, what responsibility does the majority have to undertake affirmative action on behalf of Aboriginals who do not live on-reserve?

The Question of Shared Citizenship

Prior to the mid-twentieth century, Registered Indians were denied certain basic rights: to vote in Canadian elections, for example, they were required to abandon their status as Indians. Today, Aboriginals, like all Canadians, are beneficiaries of the 1982 Charter of Rights and Freedoms. The Charter assures certain rights — including the right to vote. This affirmation of equality is not, however, as straightforward as it may seem. The Charter imposes obligations on Aboriginal governments that, on occasion, run counter to tribal traditions. For example, the Charter assures a greater measure of formal equality between the sexes than formerly prevailed, and it limits the ability of tribal governments to sanction the behaviour of individual band members who transgress tribal customs.

Two broad policy domains stand out as being in need of a strengthening of formal equality among all Canadians: health and taxation. In both these areas, a phasing out of Aboriginal special status should, I suggest, figure in the exercise of defining limits.

Health Services

The provision of health care appeared in the report of the commissioners responsible for negotiating Treaty 8. Many treaties contain a "medicine chest" clause stipulating that the federal government would provide necessary medical services, and for more than a century Ottawa has organized and financed a system of health services for Registered Indians. That system has evolved separately from the provincial systems that serve other Canadians. Given the importance of universal access to core health services in the Canadian identity since the 1960s, maintaining a separate Aboriginal system of health insurance is symbolically dubious in modern Canada.

Chiefs and councils interpret a separate system for Indians as a treaty right. Many officials in Ottawa disagree, and interpret the means of delivery and range of insured services to be discretionary policy decisions. In general, the Aboriginal system covers more services than the provincial equivalents. This second tier of health insurance invites resentment among non-Aboriginals. Its duplication of provincial health programs also introduces needless administrative costs and inefficiencies. As I discussed at some length in Chapter 3, the optimal reform here is, I believe, integration of reserve-based health programming with that afforded by the provinces to other Canadians.

Tax Exemption

Exemption from payment of federal taxes by Registered Indians living on-reserve is a longstanding provision of the *Indian Act* (section 87). Aboriginal claims for exemption from tax rely on the argument that non-Aboriginals expropriated Aboriginal lands and, in exchange, made promises — embodied in treaties and other contemporary documents — that Indians would be able to govern themselves on-reserve and remain independent of non-Aboriginal society. Furthermore, tax exemption has no doubt induced some economic activity to locate on-reserve rather than elsewhere. And, it is argued, given the limited employment opportunities on most reserves, the imposition of taxes would raise little revenue.

Two counterarguments should prevail, however, in my opinion. First, the potential for inefficient tax evasion has become too large to ignore. Relative to the late nineteenth and early twentieth centuries, when precedents were first set, the past half-century has entailed a great increase in market activity by on-reserve Indians and dramatic increases in overall rates of taxation and, although impossible to document, increased rates of evasion. Where reserves exist in close proximity to non-Aboriginal communities, the emergence of some new tax-avoidance venture creates immediate and unexpected economic losses for non-Aboriginal businesses and government treasuries. Separating legitimate, nontaxable on-reserve activities from those that are not has become an administratively costly activity, particularly for the finance ministries of the four western provinces.

The second counterargument is that the tax exemption damages the redistributive ethos that underlies all modern welfare states.

Since the nineteenth century, when most of the treaties were written, the range of publicly provided services has expanded vastly for all Canadians. So, too, has the range of taxes required to pay for them. To Canadians, the provision of these services is important. They equalize incomes and life chances, and the imposition of a moderately progressive tax system further equalizes after-tax incomes. Although most on-reserve Indians have low incomes and would be liable for little income tax, the few with relatively high incomes should take part in this redistributive process. To continue to allow otherwise contributes to a corrosive interracial irritant.

The Question of Band Council Spending and Taxation Powers

Here, I address the "plus" component of Cairns's "citizens plus." When it comes to services, bands can be expected to provide those traditionally associated with small municipalities. Band councils, however, are not just municipal governments. Ottawa and reserve-based Aboriginal leaders need to think anew about band responsibilities for education and social assistance and about the introduction of own-source taxation.

Education

If the concept of "plus" is to have meaning, reserve communities should be able to organize on-reserve school systems and use them as a means to transmit Aboriginal culture from one generation to the next. Canada has a long history of accommodating the interest of certain minority communities, defined by religion and language, in controlling local schools. Confederation would have been impossible without section 93 of the *British North America Act*, which entrenched the power of Quebec bishops over the management of Roman Catholic education in that province. Debates over granting analogous powers for Roman Catholics and francophones elsewhere in Canada have at times been contentious. But reasonable compromises have been worked out.

Education from kindergarten to grade 12 is about more than transmission of culture, however — it must also permit mastery of the basic academic skills and knowledge necessary for participation in a technical industrial society. A relevant precedent here is the concern among Québécois in the mid-twentieth century over their schools. At the time, although francophone Roman Catholic schools were preserving language and culture, they were not graduating students able to match the level displayed by anglophone students, either in Quebec or elsewhere in Canada. Quebec's Quiet Revolution closed that gap. Since that time, the link between a good education and a good job has become even tighter. The education levels of on-reserve Aboriginals, while better than at the time of the 1969 White Paper, remain far below those of non-Aboriginals and effectively bar most on-reserve children from access to well-paying jobs. For those who want a traditional lifestyle, this may not much matter. But better schools are a prerequisite if their children are to entertain a realistic choice between living on- or off-reserve. Moreover, as the Auditor General of Canada has repeatedly noted, the Department of Indian Affairs has failed even to assess academic standards in on-reserve schools, let alone insist on better performance.

Reconciling band control with higher school standards will not be easy. Reform requires greater professionalism in school administration. That, in turn, will almost certainly require individual bands to cede authority over schools to larger organizations such as tribal councils or to new, province-wide Aboriginal school boards, and that reserve schools integrate curricula and student testing more closely with the relevant province. In unduly ambiguous terms, the First Ministers and national Aboriginal leaders acknowledged as much at their 2005 meeting in Kelowna.[1]

---

1   The communique from the meeting included the following: "The Government of Canada will invest $1.05 billion over the next 5 years to promote education innovation on-reserve, including assistance to establish a network of First Nations school systems, with regional school authorities administered under First Nations jurisdictions and enhancements for First Nations basic education services" (Canada 2005b, 2).

Social Assistance

Prosperous industrial societies consider financial aid to the destitute a core social program. On-reserve, band members receive benefits administered by band councils. Off-reserve, band members are treated as are other potential beneficiaries. The rules and benefit levels are administered by the relevant provincial government.

Over the past decade, the trend in professionally well managed social assistance programs in Canada, the United States, the United Kingdom, and Scandinavia has been to place more meaningful work or training obligations on those seeking benefits, thus rejecting the idea of welfare as an entitlement equivalent to, say, universal health insurance. Underlying this trend is the conclusion that long-term welfare dependency induces a "culture of poverty" with undesirable intergenerational effects on families. Canadian social workers have accepted this thesis more tentatively than their US or UK counterparts. Nevertheless, since the mid-1990s, all provinces have turned away from entitlements and have reduced eligibility among those deemed employable. Aboriginal band councils, however, have undergone no such shift.

Arguably, the rules governing access to social assistance should be the same for all Canadians, regardless of racial identity. To achieve this, Aboriginal social assistance could be integrated with provincial social assistance programs. Such a reform would mean that professional social workers, most probably non-Aboriginal, determine who is eligible for on-reserve social assistance. Integration with provincial social assistance would also mean tightening welfare eligibility requirements. On many isolated reserves, there are few jobs other than those linked to the band council. Ease of access to social assistance permits people to remain on-reserve, while being denied social assistance is a powerful incentive to migrate off-reserve.

The policy nettle to grasp is whether Aboriginal access to on-reserve welfare solely on the basis of financial need is a treaty entitlement. Currently, band councils believe it is. Many officials in Ottawa quietly disagree — as they do about a separate Aboriginal health system — and consider the transfer to band councils of management over welfare policy to be an administrative decision by the Department of Indian Affairs.

Moscovitch and Webster (1995, 229–30) pose several reform options, ranging from administration by the provinces to administration by a national commission headed by a board composed of on-reserve registered Indians. A compromise I tentatively propose is to withdraw from individual bands the authority to distribute welfare and to entrust the function, with an accompanying budget, to an intertribal social assistance agency for each province. Agencies would face pressure to continue accommodating very high on-reserve welfare use. However, if they were large enough to hire professional social workers, they could bring more professionalism to welfare disbursements and eliminate welfare administration as a potential instrument of band political patronage. Agencies could also engage Aboriginal leaders in the more general issues of excessive reliance on welfare.

Own-Source Taxation

In his discussion of the Nisga'a Treaty, Gibson (1999, 169) praises the Nisga'a tradition of leadership as an "honourable one." But, he warns, it is disturbing to establish a template for modern Aboriginal government that relies almost exclusively on honour among on-reserve elites and envisions few checks and balances.

One of the most robust generalizations to make about the quality of governance is that it is usually poor when the government in question is not constrained by taxpayers' debating how and how much to tax themselves. The need to tax does not guarantee good government, but the absence of need to tax usually guarantees bad government. When a government must rely on own-source taxation — in other words, when those under its purview must agree to tax themselves for the services they receive — there arise highly desirable incentives for efficiency and popular participation. Since political leaders must persuade citizens to pay taxes sufficient to cover the cost of expenditures, political leaders are more likely to assess the benefit of incremental services against the cost of incremental taxation. Since citizens are collectively liable for the cost of public services, they are more likely to participate in debating the issues at hand.

By 2002, concern over the quality of band governance had become sufficiently prominent that the Department of Indian Affairs launched the First Nations Governance Initiative, accompanied by a draft bill intended to codify band council practices. Leaders of the Assembly of First Nations protested, alleging the bill to be an unwarranted intrusion on the Aboriginal right to self-government. The bill was tabled in Parliament but never enacted.

Jean Allard, former Manitoba politician and member of Ed Schreyer's New Democratic Party government, was among those whose criticism of band governance provided justification for the First Nations Governance Initiative. His manuscript is a major indictment of the status quo:

> [C]hiefs and councils today have a great deal of money to work with. The funds for housing, welfare, education and other such services flow through their hands. Since there is not real separation between politics and administration on reserves, everything on a reserve that is in any way related to band administration is politicized. Whoever is elected is in control of just about everything on a reserve. The result is elections coloured by bitter rivalries and ugly disputes.
>
> Reserves are one-dimensional systems. Elsewhere in Canadian society, multiple voices act as checks and balances on each other.... There are no such "other voices" on reserves, leaving the single dimension of politics in which to work out solutions to social, economic and political problems....
>
> On the reserves, the chiefs and councils who played ball with Indian Affairs obtained [as years passed] more and more control over budgets and services. But the checks and balances to keep the chiefs and councils on the straight and narrow were not here. People could not pick up and go to a band with a better administration. And since the money funding the band did not come from

band members, they had no means to hold their chiefs and councils accountable. (Allard 2002, 128, 131.)

Some defend the status quo by comparing Ottawa's fiscal transfers to bands to the system of fiscal federalism that underlies the provision of core social programs by the provinces. Ottawa provides funds to enable band councils to provide services of reasonable quality, and does the same for "have-not" provinces via equalization grants. A crucial difference between the two transfer systems is that equalization grants are calculated on the expectation that the recipient provinces undertake taxing efforts comparable to the average prevailing among all provinces. Even in those provinces most dependent on equalization, own-source taxation generates the majority of provincial revenues.

Admittedly, most reserves have a small tax base and offer little potential for own-source taxation. Allard proposes an interesting means to rectify this: pay a sizable portion of federal transfers not to bands but to individual Indians. The so-called numbered treaties, covering bands from western Ontario to the northern territories, provide for annual payments to individuals. At the time these treaties were negotiated in the nineteenth century, these amounts were small but not trivial. Allard proposes significant increases in the amounts paid.[2] If, for example, Indian Affairs were to disburse $2,500 annually to every adult Registered Indian, whether living on- or off-reserve, the gross cost would be about $1.4 billion. The net cost, after reducing transfers to bands by the amount paid to on-reserve Indians, would be about half. (Other compressions in the Indian Affairs budget could render the reform neutral in terms of departmental spending.)

Such a reform would pose complex administrative problems, but the benefits make it attractive. Own-source taxation would arise as bands taxed back some portion of treaty money from on-reserve

---

2   For a more extensive discussion of Allard's "updated treaty money" proposal, see Richards (2003). This article also summarizes provisions of the now-abandoned *First Nations Governance Act*.

members. The reform would also have the important virtue of lowering the excessive locational bias of present Indian Affairs transfers. Virtually all present benefits accrue to Indians if, and only if, they remain on-reserve.

The Question of Affirmative Action

What responsibility does the majority have to undertake affirmative action on behalf of Aboriginals who do not live on-reserve? The answer to this question is simple: a great deal. The key here is the education reform options discussed at length in Chapter 4. None of them will be possible, however, without the provinces' commitment to target outcomes. At the First Ministers' meeting in Kelowna in 2005, the premiers collectively committed themselves to closing the gap between K–12 education outcomes of Aboriginal and non-Aboriginal children by 2016. This augurs well, but it remains for the moment no more than a promise. It lacks the practical education programs required to give it substance.

Conclusion

Alan Cairns is right to insist that Aboriginal nationalism cannot solve Aboriginal problems by "an exaggerated stress on 'otherness'" — neither could nationalist movements among minority Québécois or African Americans. This does not mean that Canada need adopt the French tradition of *laïcité*. It does, however, mean a better affirmation of some fundamental shared aspects of citizenship. Defining the limits of Québécois nationalism required the majority outside Quebec to accept the legitimacy of that province's language laws. It also required Québécois to accept an end to many *ad hoc* fiscal transfers that disproportionately favoured their province. Something analogous is required for Aboriginals.

Aboriginal policy requires, on the one hand, a compromise between the requirements of shared citizenship and the "plus" that Aboriginals expect and, on the other, a pragmatic exercise by federal, provincial, and band-based Aboriginal leaders to put in place better social programs. The core outcomes to monitor are education, health, and employment. The links among education levels, employment rates, and reasonable incomes are intuitively obvious. They exist for Aboriginals as for other Canadians. Employment, in particular, matters in ways beyond the relief of poverty — low employment is probably a major culprit in any explanation of remaining gaps between Aboriginal and non-Aboriginal health outcomes.

Allan Blakeney has noted that Aboriginals "experience a sense of place" on-reserve, something often lost when they move away. To enhance that sense of place, lawyers will continue to negotiate new treaties and litigate the interpretation of existing treaties, activities that can help assure that Aboriginal cultural distinctness will not be abandoned. At the same time, political leaders — both Aboriginal and non-Aboriginal — must accept the reality that Aboriginals increasingly are choosing to live off-reserve. No matter where they live, Aboriginals and their children should have options that are as broad and attractive as those available to other Canadians.

There is much to be done.

References

Allard, J. 2002. "Big Bear's Treaty." Excerpt from unpublished manuscript with foreword by Gordon Gibson. *Inroads* 11: 108–69.

Antecol, H., and K. Bedard. 2002. "The Relative Earnings of Young Mexican, Black, and White Women." *Industrial and Labor Relations Review* 56 (1): 122–35.

Bishop, J. 1997. "The Effect of National Standards and Curriculum-Based External Exams on Student Achievement." *American Economic Review* 87 (2): 260–64.

———. 2000. "Privatizing Education: Lessons from Canada, Europe, and Asia." In *Vouchers and the Provision of Public Services*, edited by C. Steuerle, V. Ooms, G. Peterson, and R. Reischauer. Washington, DC: Brookings Institution Press.

———. 2001. "A Steeper, Better Road to Graduation." *Education Next* (Winter); available at web site: http://www.educationnext.org/20014/56.html.

Boothe, P. 1998. *Finding a Balance: Renewing Canadian Fiscal Federalism*. Benefactors Lecture. Toronto: C.D. Howe Institute.

Borland, M. and R. Howsen. 1992. "Students' Academic Achievement and the Degree of Market Concentration in Education." *Economics of Education Review* 11 (1): 31–39.

Bradbury, K. 2002. "Education and Wages in the 1980s and 1990s: Are All Groups Moving Up Together?" *New England Economic Review* (1st Quarter): 19–46.

British Columbia. 2003. *How Are We Doing? Demographics and Performance of Aboriginal Students in BC Public Schools 2002–2003*. Victoria: Ministry of Education. Available at web site: www.gov.bc.ca/abed

Cairns, A. 2000. *Citizens Plus: Aboriginal Peoples and the Canadian State*. Vancouver: UBC Press.

Cairns, A., and T. Flanagan. 2001. "An Exchange." *Inroads* 10: 101–22.

Canada. 1966–67. *A Survey of the Contemporary Indians of Canada*, 2 v. Ottawa: Queen's Printer; also known as the Hawthorn Report; available at web site: http://www.ainc-inac.gc.ca/pr/pub/srvy/sci_e.html.

———. 1969. "Statement of the Government of Canada on Indian Policy." Presented to Parliament by the Hon. Jean Chrétien, Minister of Indian Affairs and Northern Development. Ottawa: Department of Indian Affairs.

———. 1980. *Indian Conditions: A Survey*. Ottawa: Department of Indian and Northern Affairs.

———. 1996. *People to People, Nation to Nation: Highlights from the Report of the Royal Commission on Aboriginal Peoples*. Ottawa: Royal Commission on Aboriginal Peoples.

———. 1999. *A Second Diagnostic on the Health of First Nations and Inuit People in Canada*. Ottawa: Health Canada; available at web site: http://www.hc-sc.gc.ca.

———. 2000a. *Diabetes among Aboriginal People in Canada: The Evidence*. Ottawa: Health Canada; available at web site: http://www.hc-sc.gc.ca.

———. 2000b. "Indian and Northern Affairs Canada: Elementary and Secondary Education." Chap. 4 of *The Report of the Auditor General of Canada*. Ottawa; available at web site: www.oag-bvg.gc.ca.

———. 2002a. *Building on Values: The Future of Health Care in Canada*. Ottawa: Commission on the Future of Health Care in Canada; also known as the Romanow Commission; available at web site: http://www.hc-sc.gc.ca/english/care/romanow/indedx1.html.

———. 2002b. *Non-Insured Health Benefits Program: 2001–2002 Annual Report*. Ottawa: Health Canada; available at web site: http://www.hc-sc.ca/fnhib-dgspni.

———. 2003a. *A Statistical Profile on the Health of First Nations in Canada*. Ottawa: Health Canada; available at web site: http://www.hc-sc.gc.ca/fnihb

———. 2003b. *Aboriginal Peoples of Canada: A Demographic Profile*. Cat. no. 96F0030XIE2001007. Ottawa: Statistics Canada.

———. 2003c. *Aboriginal Peoples Survey*; selected files available on CD-ROM. Ottawa: Statistics Canada.

———. 2003d. *Urban Aboriginal Youth: An Action Plan for Change*. Final Report of the Senate Standing Committee on Aboriginal Peoples; Senator Thelma Chalifoux, chair; available at web site: http://www.parl.gc.ca/37/2/parl-bus/commbus/senate/com-e/abor-e/rep-e/repfinoct03-e.htm.

———. 2004a. *2001 Aboriginal Peoples Survey Community Profiles*. Ottawa: Statistics Canada; available at web site: http://www12.statcan.ca/english/profil01/PlaceSearchForm1.cfm.

———. 2004b. *Basic Departmental Data, 2003*. Ottawa: Department of Indian Affairs and Northern Development.

———. 2004c. "Indian and Northern Affairs Canada — Education Program and Post-Secondary Student Support." Chap. 5 of *The Report of the Auditor General of Canada*. Ottawa; available at web site: http://www.oag-bvd.gc.ca

———. 2004d. *HIV/AIDS among Aboriginal Peoples in Canada: A Continuing Concern*. Ottawa: Public Health Agency of Canada; available at web site: http://www.phac-aspc.gc.ca/publicat/epiu-aepi/epi_update_may_04/9_e.html.

———. 2005a. *Aboriginal Peoples Living Off-Reserve in Western Canada: Estimates from the Labour Force Survey, April 2004–March 2005*. Cat. no. 71-587-XIE. Ottawa: Statistics Canada; available at web site: http://www.statcan.ca/english/freepub/71-587-XIE/71-587-XIE2005001.pdf.

———. 2005b. "Government of Canada invests in immediate action to improve lives of Aboriginal peoples in Canada." Press release, November 25; available at web site: http://www.pm.gc.ca/eng/news.asp?id=661

———. 2005c. "Readmission to Saskatchewan Correctional Services among Aboriginal and Non-Aboriginal Adults." *The Daily* (Statistics Canada), June 3; available at web site: http://www.statcan.ca/Daily/English/050603/d050603a.htm.

———. 2005d. "Strengthening Relationships and Closing the Gap." Paper released at First Ministers' and National Aboriginal Leaders' Meeting, Kelowna, BC, November; available at web site: http://www.ainc-inac.gc.ca/nr/iss/fmm_e.html.

Chandler, M., and C. Lalonde. 1998. "Cultural Continuity as a Hedge against Suicide in Canada's First Nations." *Transcultural Psychiatry* 35 (2): 191–219.

Cook, M., and W. Evans. 2000. "Families or Schools? Explaining the Convergence in White and Black Academic Performance." *Journal of Labor Economics* 18 (4): 729–54.

Coon Come, M. 2003. "Assembly of First Nations national chief expresses disappointment with Federal Court of Appeal ruling on Treaty 8 tax promise"; available at web site: http://www.afn.ca/Media/2003/june/june_11_03.htm.

Cornell, S., and J. Kalt. 1998. "Sovereignty and Nation-Building: The Development Challenge in Indian Country Today." *American Indian Culture and Research Journal* 22 (3): 187–214.

Cowley, P., and S. Easton. 2004. *Report Card on Aboriginal Education in British Columbia*, 2004 ed. Vancouver: Fraser Institute.

Cutler, D., E. Glaeser, and J. Shapiro. 2003. "Why Have Americans Become More Obese?" *Journal of Economic Perspectives* 17 (3): 93–116.

Drolet, M. 2002. "New Evidence on Gender Pay Differentials: Does Measurement Matter?" *Canadian Public Policy* 28 (1): 1–16.

Drost, H., and J. Richards. 2003. "Income On- and Off-Reserve: How Aboriginals Are Faring." *C.D. Howe Institute Commentary* 175. Toronto: C.D. Howe Institute.

Evans, W., and R. Schwab. 1995. "Finish High School and Starting College: Do Catholic Schools Make a Difference?" *Quarterly Journal of Economics* 110 (4): 947–74.

Flanagan, T. 2000. *First Nations? Second Thoughts*. Montreal; Kingston: McGill-Queen's University Press.

Florence, J., and B. Yeager. 1999. "Treatment of Type 2 Diabetes Mellitus." *American Family Physician*, May 15.

George, D. 1970. "My Very Good Dear Friends…" In *The Only Good Indian, Essays by Canadian Indians*, ed. Waubageshig. Toronto: New Press.

Gibson, G. 1999. "A Principled Analysis of the Nisga'a Treaty." *Inroads* 8: 165–78.

Greene, J., P. Peterson, and J. Du. 1996. *The Effectiveness of School Choice in Milwaukee: A Secondary Analysis of Data from the Program's Evaluation*. Cambridge, Mass.: Harvard University Press.

Hanushek, E. 2002. "Publicly Provided Education." NBER Working Paper 8799. Cambridge, Mass.: National Bureau of Economic Research.

Howe, E. 2002. "Education and Lifetime Income for Aboriginal People in Saskatchewan." Unpublished working paper, Department of Economics, University of Saskatchewan.

Indian Chiefs of Alberta. 1970. *Citizens Plus: A Presentation by the Indian Chiefs of Alberta to the Right Honourable P.-E. Trudeau*. The Red Paper, prepared under direction of Harold Cardinal. Edmonton: Indian Association of Alberta.

King, T. 2003. *The Truth about Stories: A Native Narrative*. Toronto: House of Anansi.

Ladd, H., and E. Fiske. 2001. "The Uneven Playing Field of School Choice: Evidence from New Zealand." *Journal of Policy Analysis and Management* 20 (1): 43–64.

Léger & Léger. 2005. "Quebec Survey." Opinon poll commissioned by *Le Journal de Montréal* and *The Gazette*, May 14.

McRae, D., and P. Pearse. 2004. *Treaties and Transition: Towards a Sustainable Fishery on Canada's Pacific Coast*. Report prepared for the Federal-Provincial Post Treaty Fisheries Joint Task Group. Ottawa: Department of Fisheries and Oceans.

Matas, R., and R. Mickleburgh. 2002. "Most in BC survey believe referendum harms treaty talks." *Globe and Mail* (Toronto). April 18, pp. A1, A8.

Moffitt, R. 2003. "The Negative Income Tax and the Evolution of US Welfare Policy." *Journal of Economic Perspectives* 17 (7): 119–40.

Morbidity and Mortality Weekly Report (MMWR). 1997. "Trends in the Prevalence and Incidence of Self-Reported Diabetes Mellitus — United States, 1980–1994." 44 (43): 1014–18, October 31.

———. 2003. "Diabetes Prevalence among American Indians and Alaska Natives and the Overall Population." 52 (30): 702–04, August 1.

Moscovitch, A., and A. Webster. 1995. "Aboriginal Social Assistance Expenditures." In *How Ottawa Spends, 1995–96: Mid-Life Crisis*, edited by S. Phillips. Ottawa: Carleton University Press.

Neal, D. 1997. "The Effects of Catholic Secondary Schooling on Educational Achievement." *Journal of Labor Economics* 15 (1): 98–123.

Norris, D., A. Siggner, and R. Costa. 2003. "What the Census and *The Aboriginal Peoples Survey* Tell Us about Aboriginal Conditions in Canada." Paper presented at the Aboriginal Strategies Conference, Edmonton, October.

OECD (Organisation for Economic Co-operation and Development). 1996. *Employment Outlook* 62. Paris: OECD.

Pendakur, K., and R. Pendakur. 2002. "Colour My World: Have Earnings Gaps for Canadian-Born Ethnic Minorities Changed Over Time?" *Canadian Public Policy* 28 (4): 489–512.

Ponting, J., and R. Gibbins. 1980. *Out of Irrelevance*. Scarborough: Butterworth.

Richards, J. 2001. "Neighbors Matter: Poor Neighborhoods and Urban Aboriginal Policy." *C.D. Howe Institute Commentary* 156. Toronto: C.D. Howe Institute.

———. 2002. "Indian/Non-Indian Life Expectancy: Why the Gap?" *Inroads* 12: 48–59.

———. 2003. "A New Agenda for Strengthening Canada's Aboriginal Populations: Individual Treaty Benefits, Reduced Transfers to Bands and Own-Source Taxation." *Backgrounder* 66. Toronto: C.D. Howe Institute.

———. 2005. "Labour Markets and Social Policy: A Qualified Agenda for the Future." In *Prospects for Canada: Progress and Challenges Twenty Years after the Macdonald Commission*, edited by D. Laidler and W. Robson. Toronto: C.D. Howe Institute.

Richards, J., and A. Vining. 2004. "Aboriginal Off-Reserve Education: Time for Action." *C.D. Howe Institute Commentary* 198. Toronto: C.D. Howe Institute.

Rouse, C. 1998. "Schools and Student Achievement: More Evidence from the Milwaukee Parental Choice Program." *Economic Policy Review* 4 (1): 61–78.

Sawhill, I., and S. Smith. 2000. "Vouchers for Elementary and Secondary Education." In *Vouchers and the Provision of Public Services*, edited by C. Steuerle, V. Ooms, G. Peterson, and R. Reischauer. Washington, DC: Brookings Institution Press.

Scott, D. [1905] 1991. "The Forsaken." In *Poets of the Confederation*, edited by M. Ross. Toronto: McClelland & Stewart.

Siggner, A., and R. Costa. 2005. *Aboriginal Conditions in Census Metropolitan Areas, 1981–2001*. Ottawa: Statistics Canada; available at web site: http://www.statcan.ca/ english/research/89-613-MIE/89-613-MIE2005008.pdf.

Sparklingeyes, P. 2005. "Aboriginal Learning Services, Edmonton Catholic Schools"; available at web site: http://www.sfu.ca/mpp/aboriginal/colloquium.

Steele, S. 2002. "The Age of White Guilt and the Disappearance of the Black Individual." *Harper's Magazine*, November, pp. 33–42.

Steffenhagen, J. 2003. "East pupils meet west schools." *Vancouver Sun*, June 2, pp. B1, B7.

Tjepkema, M. 2002. *The Health of the Off-reserve Aboriginal Population*. Cat. no. 82-003. Ottawa: Statistics Canada.

Trudeau, P.-E. [1964] 1968. "Separatist Counter-Revolutionaries." *Federalism and the French Canadians*. Toronto: Macmillan of Canada. [Reprinted and translated from the original in *Cité libre*.]

Tuomilehto, J., et al. 2001. "Prevention of Type 2 Diabetes Mellitus by Changes in Lifestyle among Subjects with Impaired Glucose Tolerance." *New England Journal of Medicine* 344 (18): 1343–50.

United Nations. 2004. *Human Development Indicators*; available at web site: http://www.undp.org/hdr2003/indicator.

Weiher, G., and K. Tedin. 2002. "Does Choice Lead to Racially Distinctive Schools? Charter Schools and Household Preferences." *Journal of Policy Analysis and Management* 21 (1): 79–92.

Witte, J. 2000. *The Market Approach to Education: An Analysis of America's First Voucher Program*. Princeton, NJ: Princeton University Press.

WHO (World Health Organization). 2004. *Prevention of Mental Disorders: Effective Interventions and Policy Options*. Summary report. Geneva: WHO; available at web site: http://www.who.int/mental_health/evidence/en.

Young, T., E. Szathmary, S. Evers, and B. Wheatley. 1990. "Geographical Distribution of Diabetes Mellitus among the Native Population of Canada: A National Survey." *Social Science and Medicine* 31 (2): 129–39.

Young, T., J. Reading, B. Elias, and J. O'Neil. 2000. "Type 2 Diabetes Mellitus in Canada's First Nations: Status of an Epidemic in Progress." *Canadian Medical Association Journal* 163 (5); available at web site: http://www.cmaj.ca.

Zanzig, B. 1997. "Measuring the Impact of Competition in Local Government Education Markets on the Cognitive Achievement of Students." *Economics of Education Review* 16 (4): 431–41.

About the Author

John Richards grew up in Saskatchewan, and served as a member of Allan Blakeney's government in the early 1970s. He is trained as an economist, and is a member of the faculty in the new Simon Fraser University Public Policy Program. He has written extensively on social policy in Canada, primarily via the C.D. Howe Institute, where he holds the Roger Phillips chair in social policy. His current social policy focus is on Aboriginal policy.

He co-edits (with Henry Milner) *Inroads*, a Canadian policy journal — see www.inroadsjournal.ca. In addition, over the past decade he has undertaken teaching and research in Bangladesh. He heads the Centre for Policy Research, an institute linked to the International University of Business Agriculture and Technology — see www.iubat.edu/cpr. The Centre's most recent publication is *Energy Policy for Bangladesh* (co-authored with Professor Alimullah Miyan), a response to the National Energy Policy published by the government of Bangladesh in spring 2004.

Members of the
C.D. Howe Institute*

---

* The views expressed in this publication are those of the author, and do not necessarily represent the opinions of the Institute's Board of Directors or members.

Canadian Chemical Producers'
Association
Canadian Energy Pipeline Association
Canadian Federation of Independent
Business
Canadian Finance & Leasing
Association
Canadian Imperial Bank of Commerce
The Canadian Institute of Chartered
Accountants
Canadian Life and Health Insurance
Association Inc.
Canadian Manufacturers & Exporters
Canadian Oil Sands Limited
Canadian Pacific Railway
Canadian Pension Plan Investment
Board
Canadian Tax Foundation
Canadian Tire Corporation, Limited
Canadian Western Bank
Canam Group Inc.
Candor Investments Ltd.
Cangene Corporation
CanWest Global Communications Corp.
Cargill Limited
Carleton University
Catalyst Paper Corporation
The CCL Group Inc.
Ken Chapman
CHC Helicopter Corporation
Ben Cherniavsky
Kenneth Christoffel
Clairvest Group Inc.
CMA Holdings Inc.
CN
Jack Cockwell
Cogeco Inc.
Marshall A. Cohen
CompCorp
Concordia University
ConocoPhillips Canada
E. Kendall Cork

Marcel Côté
Glen Cronkwright
Paul R. Curley
Thomas P. d'Aquino
Catherine A. Delaney
Deloitte & Touche LLP
Ildiko K. Dereza
Desjardins Ducharme LLP
Deutsche Bank AG, Canada Branch
Steven Devries
Wendy Dobson
Dofasco Inc.
Domtar Inc.
Donner Canadian Foundation
Duke Energy Gas Transmission Canada
E.I. du Pont Canada Company
Janet Ecker
John F. Eckert
Economap Inc.
Edco Financial Holdings Ltd.
Edmonton Economic Development
Corporation
E-L Financial Corporation Limited
Elk Valley Coal Corp.
Emera Inc.
William F. Empey
Enbridge
EnCana Corporation
Energy Council of Canada
Enerplus Resources Fund
Ensign Resource Service Group Inc.
Ensis Growth Fund Inc.
Ernst & Young LLP
Morrey M. Ewing
Export Development Canada
Fairmont Hotels and Resorts
Falconbridge Limited
Fednav Limited
John T. Ferguson
Fidelity Investments
Finning International Inc.
Aaron Fish

James D. Fleck
Ford Motor Company of Canada,
  Limited
Forest Products Association of Canada
Robert and Julia Foster
Four Halls Inc.
Four Seasons Hotels Limited
Fraser Milner Casgrain LLP
Fraser Papers Inc.
Gaz Métro
GE Canada
General Motors of Canada Limited
Gibson Energy Ltd.
Christine Girvan
Gluskin Sheff + Associates Inc.
Goal Group of Companies
Goldberg Group
Goodmans LLP
Peter Goring
John A.G. Grant
James K. Gray
Greater Saskatoon Chamber of
  Commerce
The Great-West Life Assurance Company,
  London Life Insurance Company
  and Canada Life
John Haag
Geoffrey Hale
Harvard Developments Inc., A Hill
  Company
G.R. Heffernan
Lawrence Herman
Hill & Knowlton
Historica Foundation
Hollinger Inc.
William L. Holt
Honeywell Canada
HSBC Bank Canada
HSD Partners Inc.
H. Douglas Hunter
Hydro-Québec Production
Lou Hyndman, Q.C.

IBM Canada Ltd.
Imperial Oil Limited
Imperial Tobacco Canada Limited
Inco Limited
Industrial Alliance Life Insurance
  Company
Information Services Corporation of
  Saskatchewan
The Institute for Competitiveness and
  Prosperity
Insurance Bureau of Canada
Inter Pipeline Fund
Investment Dealers Association of
  Canada
The Investment Funds Institute of
  Canada
Investors Group
Ipsco Inc.
J.D. Irving Limited
J.P. Morgan Securities Canada Inc.
Jackman Foundation
Jarislowsky, Fraser Limited
W. Edwin Jarmain
John Dobson Foundation
Robert Johnstone
JTI-Macdonald Corp.
Juniper Fund Management
John A. Kazanjian
Thomas E. Kierans
James T. Kiernan
Frank F. Kolb
KPA Advisory Services Ltd.
KPMG LLP
Joseph Kruger II
La Jolla Resources International Ltd.
Laval University
Law Commission of Canada
R. John Lawrence
Jacques A. Lefebvre
Lehigh Inland Cement Limited
David A. Leslie
David Lindsay

Hugh D. Segal
Lindsay K. Shaddy
Sejal Shah
Gordon Sharwood
Shell Canada Limited
Sherritt International Corporation
Mary-Anne Sillamaa
Simon Fraser University
Paul G. Smith
SNC Lavalin Group Inc.
Sobeys Inc.
Philip Spencer, Q.C.
Wayne Steadman
Morley Stock
Sun Life Financial Inc.
Suncor Energy Inc.
Harry Swain
Christopher Sweeney
Thomas H.B. Symons
Syncrude Canada Limited
Tax Executives Institute, Inc.
TD Bank Financial Group
Teck Cominco Limited
Frederick H. Telmer
Tembec Inc.
The Thomson Corporation
The Toronto Board of Trade
Torstar Corporation
Torys LLP
TransAlta Corporation
TransCanada Corporation
Transcontinental Inc.

True Energy Inc.
Robert J. Turner, Q.C.
UBS Global Asset Management
   (Canada) Co.
Université de Montréal
University College of the Fraser Valley
University of Alberta
University of British Columbia
The University of Calgary
The University of Lethbridge
University of Manitoba
University of Ottawa
University of Regina
University of Saskatchewan
University of Toronto
University of Waterloo
The University of Western Ontario
G. Douglas Valentine
Via Rail Canada Inc.
W. Garfield Weston Foundation
Jack H. Warren
Watson Wyatt
Weston Forest Corp.
David J.S. Winfield
Alfred G. Wirth
Adam H. Zimmerman

Honorary Members

John Crispo
Grant L. Reuber